CARPENTRY, JOINERY AND MACHINE WOODWORKING

(Wood Trades Part 1)

A. B. Emary

F.B.I.C.C.

MACMILLAN

First edition 1974
Reprinted 1978, 1979, 1982, 1986

Published by
MACMILLAN EDUCATION LTD
Houndmills, Basingstoke, Hampshire RG21 2XS
and London
Companies and representatives
throughout the world

Printed in Hong Kong

ISBN 0–333–15463–0

Contents

Preface

This book has been written with the City and Guilds of London Institute Syllabuses for the Timber Trades (Part 1) in mind, which are intended to cover the first year of the Carpentry and Joinery and Machine Woodworking crafts.

A portion from each of the practical and theory syllabuses, together with that dealing with science, combine to make an integrated section in which students from both crafts work together, after this each craft goes more deeply into its own speciality. The integrated and the individual sections have not been separated in this book because the author feels that teachers in different colleges will work out their own schemes to cover Part 1 of this new programme. A study of Part 1 will show that very little work is covered in the integrated portion as compared with the sections that the crafts cover separately — a point which some people may regret.

Some teachers may think that the practical and technology parts of the integrated section of Part 1 can be covered in the first term of the year and that the other sections can be spread over the remaining two terms.

Courses with full-time students in the first year of their apprenticeship — who will be expected to sit for their craft examination certificate at the end of their second year at the college — will have to cover Part 1 and also a substantial part of Part 2 in the first year, so that the remaining sections of Part 2 can be covered in the second year, presumably on day release.

Teachers in some colleges with day-release students may feel that the content of Part 2 of the syllabuses presents a formidable task if it is to be covered in the last two years of a three-year course and may therefore decide to include some of the subjects of Part 2 in the first year's work.

In this book, the author is not merely trying to impart knowledge to students, but also to present problems to them to which they should find the answers from other sources, for instance, from their teacher or from their college library. The object of this exercise is to motivate the student to find out for himself.

The teaching of the use of hand tools and woodcutting machinery cannot be accomplished by means of books. The student has to handle the tools himself, get the feel of them and have their proper use demonstrated by an expert. This applies also to machinery; the woodcutting machinist must get to understand these machines thoroughly in the machine shop and handle them under expert supervision.

A book can, however, give details of tools and machines that are not apparent in the workshop. The roles of the workshop and of the machine shop in technical colleges are proficiency in the use of the tools of the trade and the production of work, but the technicalities should be left to the teacher in the classroom and to the author.

It is hoped that future books will cover the two crafts of carpentry and joinery and machine woodworking separately so that students and teachers in those crafts will be able to obtain information on the subject to which they have dedicated a large portion of their working life.

I have been assisted in the compilation of this book by some very useful information and photographs of woodcutting machinery kindly supplied by Wadkin Ltd, of Leicester.

1974   A.B.E.

1. MATERIALS

Trees are exogenous. This means that a layer of wood cells is added to the tree just below the bark each growing season, during spring and summer. New bark cells are also added to completely enclose these additional cells (figure 1.1).

The four main parts of a tree are the roots, the trunk, the branches and the leaves. Roots absorb moisture from the soil, the moisture passes upwards, through the sapwood into the trunk and branches until it enters the leaves, which turn it into food for the tree. The leaves give off oxygen and absorb carbon dioxide, which produces the sugars and starches necessary for the growth of the tree. Sunlight is also required for food production — this process is called photosynthesis.

The food then passes down through the inner layers of the bark to nourish the thin layers of cells called the cambium cells. These produce the new wood and bark cells every growing season. Any surplus food is stored in the horizontal parenchyma cells called rays (figure 1.2).

Each growing season the tree will produce fruit (seeds) which fall to the ground where they germinate and the process of growth starts again.

All trees begin to die when they have reached maturity. Some trees mature fairly early compared with others. The dying process will be seen when mature trees are felled. Decay starts from the centre of the trunk and spreads outwards.

During a tree's early years a cross-section through the trunk shows that it is mostly composed of sapwood, which gradually turns into heartwood. When the tree has reached its maturity, it is composed entirely of heartwood.

There are two types of commercial timbers — softwoods and hardwoods (figure 1.3).

Give two examples of each.

Softwoods   Hardwoods

....

....

The assumption must not be made that hardwoods are always harder than softwoods. Many softwoods are fairly hard, such as pitch pine and parana pine, and some hardwoods, such as balsa and obeche, are particularly soft.

Figure 1.4 represents a cross-section through the trunk of a tree. The various parts are marked with a letter; place that letter against each gross feature in the table below. Write a brief outline of the functions of the various parts of a tree:

Roots ....

....

....

Trunk ....

....

....

Leaves ....

....

....

Bark (inner) ....

....

....

Bark (outer) ....

....

....

Cambium cells ....

....

....

Heartwood ....

....

....

growth of a tree

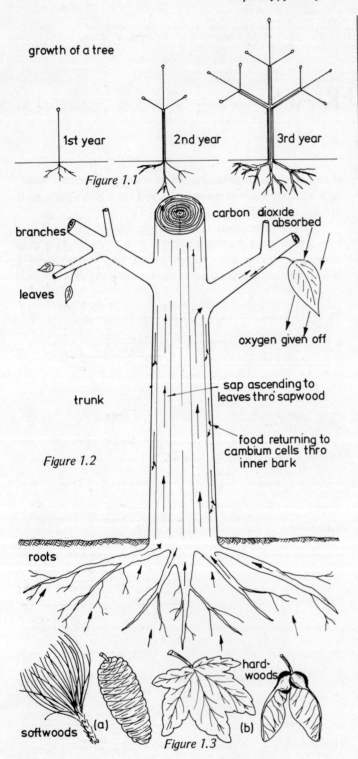

1st year   2nd year   3rd year

Figure 1.1

branches

leaves

carbon dioxide absorbed

oxygen given off

sap ascending to leaves thro' sapwood

food returning to cambium cells thro' inner bark

trunk

Figure 1.2

roots

softwoods (a)

hard-woods

Figure 1.3 (b)

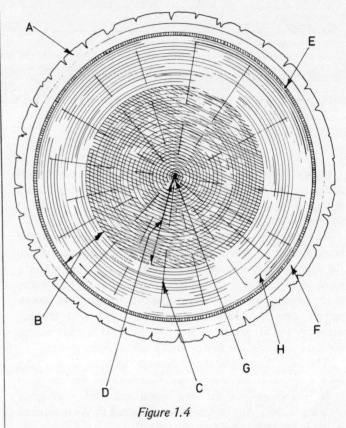

Figure 1.4

GROSS FEATURE	SHOWN BY LETTER
CAMBIUM CELLS	
INNER BARK	
SAPWOOD	
RAYS	
OUTER BARK	
GROWTH RINGS	
HEARTWOOD	
MEDULLA	

Sapwood ....

....

....

Horizontal rays ....

....

....

CONVERSION OF LOGS INTO BOARDS

When a tree has been felled, it should be transported without delay to a timber merchant so that it can be stacked correctly and seasoned before defects, such as splitting, can take place.

Logs are converted into boards either with circular saws, band-saws, etc.; this should be carried out by skilled men so that the boards obtained are sound and of the type required. A skilled machinist will produce boards from a log with a minimum of short or sloping grain, which is a weakness in timbers that are to be used for structural work.

The direction of the growth rings plays an important part in the conversion of logs. Some logs are required for boards that are to be used for joinery purposes and others are required for beams that are to carry loads, such as floor joists and roof rafters.

Figure 1.5 shows how a log would be converted for boards that are to be used for general-purpose work, for instance, first fixing timbers in houses, (roofs, etc.) and for joinery items, such as doors and windows. Boards produced in this way are a mixture of good and bad and should really be avoided for work of a specific nature.

The log shown in figure 1.6 will give boards that are termed *tangentially sawn*, which means that the wide edges of the boards are tangential to the growth rings. The growth rings run across the width of each board. These boards are fairly strong when used for floor joists and similar work because the summerwood cells from which softwoods obtain their strength are like a series of beams when the timbers are placed on edge. They are not good for joinery purposes because they tend to cup as they shrink or swell.

Figures 1.7 and 1.8 show two methods of producing *quarter sawn boards*. The growth rings run through the thickness of each board and such boards are most suitable for joinery purposes because they tend to shrink less and maintain their flatness.

Figure 1.9 shows that short-grain boards are unsuitable for many purposes, especially for structural work.

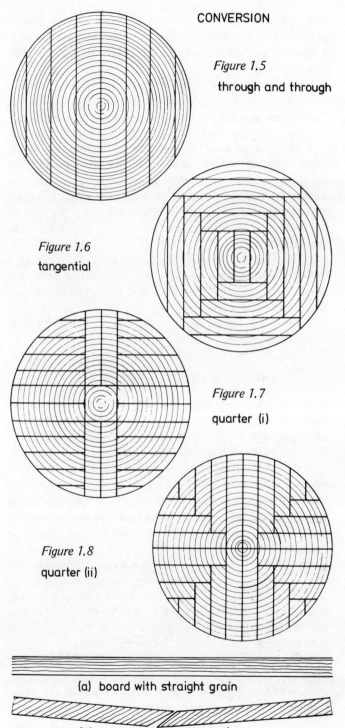

CONVERSION

Figure 1.5

through and through

Figure 1.6

tangential

Figure 1.7

quarter (i)

Figure 1.8

quarter (ii)

(a) board with straight grain

Figure 1.9   (b) board with sloping grain

THE NEED FOR SEASONING (DRYING)

When a tree is felled it contains far too much water to allow it to be used for building purposes. If it were used and placed in a building out of the weather it would shrink, split and probably twist.

Most, not all, of the water in the timber must be removed carefully if it is to remain suitable for use in joinery items. Even timber that is to be used for such work as roofs, floors, etc., must also have a certain percentage of the water removed.

If all the water were removed from the timber, the timber would start to absorb water from the atmosphere, thus increasing its size and possibly doing damage to surrounding woodwork. The amount of water that must be left in a piece of timber depends therefore on where it is to be fixed and on the amount of moisture in the surrounding atmosphere (the humidity).

If flooring or skirting boards were to be fixed in a centrally-heated house, the moisture to be left in the timber should be considerably less than that to be left in the roof rafters of that same building.

Timber can be dried in one or both ways, namely, air dried or kiln dried or both.

DRYING TIMBER

If trees that have recently been felled are left in the forest for a time before they are removed, several things can happen. In addition to the possibility of attack by some form of pest, the moisture in the timber would dry out at a very fast rate, especially if the atmosphere were dry and warm; this would result in splits occurring at the sawn ends of the logs and also around the outer surfaces. This splitting would also set up stresses in the logs, which would result in further splitting when they are cut into boards, since these stresses would be released.

Therefore people who are felling trees must arrange for the logs to be removed from the forest and transported to the sawyer's yard as quickly as possible so that they can be cut up without delay. It is much easier to dry a small piece of timber without causing degrades to appear than it is to dry a large bulk of timber.

When the logs have been converted into boards they must be dried, or, to use the correct term, *seasoned*. If this is not done carefully, the boards, even in their much smaller state, will start to dry out unevenly and splits will begin to appear on their surfaces.

Two methods are used for drying boards and these are known as air seasoning and kiln seasoning.

Air seasoning

Air seasoning requires a suitable site and a drying shed in which the boards can be stacked properly so that they can dry out evenly. Figure 1.10 shows how softwood boards should be stored to ensure even drying. Ideally, an open-sided shed with a sloping roof should be used. A flat concrete floor would also be an asset in a drying shed.

To ensure that the boards dry out evenly, an air current should be able to pass over all four surfaces of each board — hence the open-sided shed. In addition to the shed, narrow strips of wood, called *piling sticks* must be placed between each layer of board to keep the layers apart. Also, as each layer of boards is placed in position, a small space should be left between the boards. These arrangements will expose the four surfaces of each board to the air current passing through the stack.

The first layer of boards should have a fairly large space between it and the concrete floor. This can be achieved by first placing some fairly large timbers, all of the same thickness, on the floor with the first row of piling sticks on these timbers.

The boards should be supported every 600 mm or so along their lengths; hence the large timbers placed on the floor will be spaced at equal distances along the length of the stack.

The piling sticks are an important part of the stack for two reasons, namely

(i) They must be of the same type of timber as the boards in the stack. Different types can cause stains on the surfaces of the boards and this can prove to be detrimental in some cases.

(ii) The thickness of the piling sticks will control, to a certain extent, the drying rate of the boards. Thick piling sticks will allow much more air to pass through the stack than thin piling sticks; hence, the thickness of sticks to be used will depend on the capacity of the timber to give up its moisture content. These sticks are generally about 19–25 mm thick.

A good stack of boards is illustrated in figure 1.11. The piling sticks are positioned equal distances apart and are in vertical alignment. The boards have been sorted by length to ensure that they are straight when removed from the stack. The longest boards are all at the bottom and the shorter ones towards the top.

Figure 1.12 shows what could happen in a badly built stack of timber. Figure 1.13 shows on a larger scale how the boards should be stacked and figure 1.14 indicates what would happen if the several points described above were ignored.

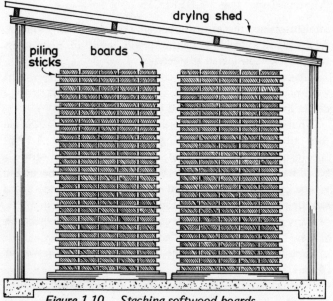

Figure 1.10   Stacking softwood boards

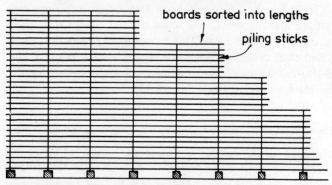

Figure 1.11   Well stacked boards

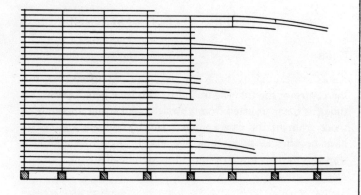

Figure 1.12   Badly stacked boards

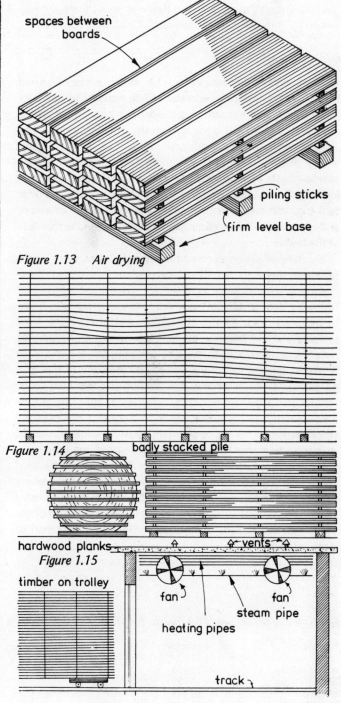

Figure 1.13   Air drying

Figure 1.14

Figure 1.15

Figure 1.16   Kiln seasoning

Figure 1.15 shows how hardwood boards should be stacked. Bear in mind that the figure or growth-ring arrangements are important in hardwoods for matching-up purposes.

Kiln seasoning

This method is considered to be much better than air seasoning. The moisture content can be reduced to any level and if this is carefully carried out it will not have any ill effects on the timber. If it is done incorrectly, splitting and twisting and even more severe degrades can result.

A kiln is a small building, usually with a rail track leading into it (figure 1.16). Inside the kiln are means for raising or lowering the level of humidity to any required level, and large fans that will force the air in the kiln to circulate clockwise or anti-clockwise. The air circulation will encourage the moisture at the timber surfaces to evaporate.

Stacking of timber is carried out in exactly the same way as for air drying.

Drying schedules are available for specific timbers and by following such a schedule — which means starting with a low temperature and a high humidity and then raising the temperature and lowering the humidity over a predetermined time — the timber can be dried to any moisture content. As it is almost impossible to dry timber to a moisture of less than 18 per cent by air drying, this method is considered to be inadequate for joinery purposes, especially as most houses now have central heating which tends to draw out the moisture from the timber to the equilibrium moisture content, that is, down to a level that is equal to the surrounding atmosphere.

Timber dried by natural means (air drying) cannot be dried efficiently because the amount of moisture in the atmosphere is always changing. The boards near the outside of an air-dried stack may be drier or wetter than those near the centre of the stack and, in any case, the moisture will never be less than 18 per cent, which is unsuitable for many joinery and carpentry items.

Moisture content of timber for specific purposes.

Purpose	Per cent
doors (exterior)	12—16
doors (interior)	10—15
windows	12—18
external cladding	16—20
roof timbers	14—18
flooring	8—15 (Depending on heating system)
joinery items	10—14

DEFECTS

Straight-grained pieces of timber are considered the strongest. Any deviation from straightness will result in a weakness that must be considered as a defect.

Figure 1.17a shows what could happen if a heavy weight were placed at the centre of a beam with very short grain, a defect that is very often caused by bad conversion.

What appears to be a board with straight grain can often turn out to be one with sloping or short grain. Figure 1.17(b) and (c) show how it is possible to ascertain whether or not a board has sloping grain. A piece of wood with a sharpened pin in one end should be dragged over the surface of the board resulting in the pin following the direction of grain.

Many defects in timber are caused by careless drying. Some of these defects are shown in figures 1.18 to 1.22.

Cupping: the edges of the boards curl up as shown in figure 1.18.

Bowing and twisting: boards curl in their length (figures 1.19 and 1.20).

When boards are ripped down their length it is sometimes noticed that the two halves at the cut end either spring apart or together (figure 1.21). This is another drying defect and is called case hardening. Honeycombing is another result of bad drying and appears as small splits or openings when the end of the plank is looked at (see figure 1.22).

Identification of defects

There are many defects in timber and almost all impair its strength in addition to reducing its usefulness for joinery purposes. Some defects, however, can be used for decorative purposes, such as burrs.

COMMON DEFECTS AFFECTING STRENGTH

Knots

Knots are caused by branches and these very often pass into the centre of the tree (figure 1.23). This weakness is caused by the cells being diverted from a straight course and thus causing short grain in the sawn timber. Dead knots are knots that have become loose in their sockets. Figures 1.24 and 1.25 show the various types of knots found in boards.

Shakes, splits and checks

Shakes are cracks that occur in the timber and run in the direction of the growth rings (figures 1.26—1.29). Cup shakes

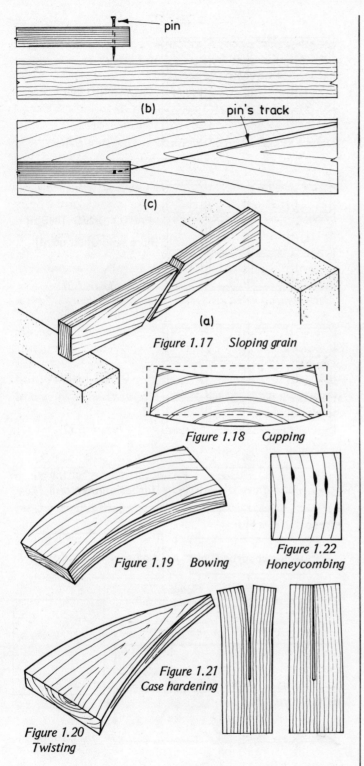

pin

(b)

pin's track

(c)

Figure 1.17   Sloping grain

(a)

Figure 1.18   Cupping

Figure 1.19   Bowing

Figure 1.22
Honeycombing

Figure 1.21
Case hardening

Figure 1.20
Twisting

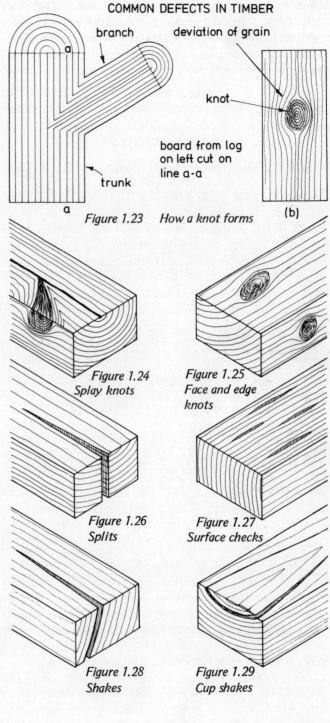

COMMON DEFECTS IN TIMBER

branch

deviation of grain

knot

trunk

board from log
on left cut on
line a-a

a

a

(b)

Figure 1.23   How a knot forms

Figure 1.24
Splay knots

Figure 1.25
Face and edge
knots

Figure 1.26
Splits

Figure 1.27
Surface checks

Figure 1.28
Shakes

Figure 1.29
Cup shakes

occur where two separate layers of growth rings fail to adhere sufficiently. Splits are cracks in the timber and travel in a radial direction across the thickness of the board. Checks are shakes that often appear on the surfaces of boards and are usually of short length. Most of the cracks in timber are caused by drying under adverse conditions. Other defects are caused by fungi and insects.

MOISTURE CONTENT

It has already been explained that a tree, when felled, contains too much water to enable the timber to be used for building purposes. If used in the green state, movement in the timber would take place. By movement we mean that the timber would shrink in size because some of the moisture would evaporate and the timber would split. To overcome this movement in the manufactured article — such as doors, windows, skirting boards and floorboards — some of the water must be removed as soon as the log is converted into boards.

When timber begins to dry out, the water moves to the surfaces of the boards and then evaporates. The first water to be released is that from the cell cavities, which is known as *free water* (see figure 1.30). No movement in the timber will occur if this water is allowed to remain in the cell cavities and also, no movement will take place during the time it is being removed from the timber. It must be realised that, in addition to the free water, there is also water present that is saturating the cell walls. There will also be no movement in the timber as long as this water remains in the walls. When all the free water has been removed the *fibre saturation point* is reached which means that although there is no free water in the cell cavities, the walls of the cells are still saturated (see figure 1.31).

Once the water in the cell walls begins to dry out, the timber starts to shrink and will continue to do so until there is no water left. If dry timber is placed in a moist atmosphere it will absorb water and this will increase the size of the timber. From this it should be concluded that we must remove only a certain amount of the moisture from the timber so that no movement will take place when it is fixed in position (figure 1.32). In other words, it must have the same moisture content as the surrounding space in which it is fixed. This moisture content is referred to as *equilibrium moisture content*.

In Britain the moisture content in the atmosphere can fluctuate considerably so that a piece of damp timber placed in a dry position can start to decrease in size because the moisture in the atmosphere decreases (figure 1.33a(i) and (ii)). The reverse is also the case (figure 1.33b(i) and (ii)). To overcome this movement the timber will have to be sealed by

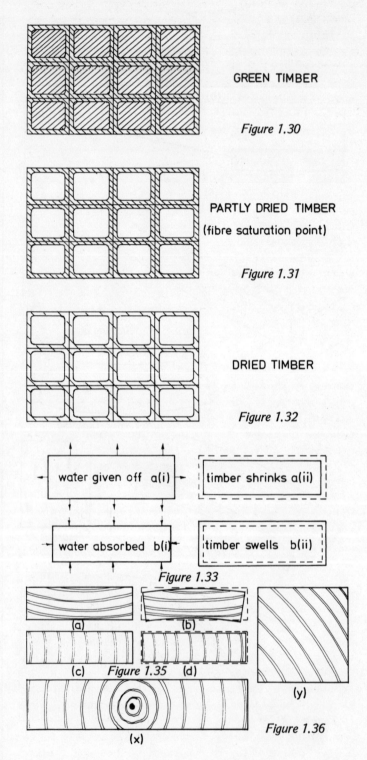

GREEN TIMBER

Figure 1.30

PARTLY DRIED TIMBER

(fibre saturation point)

Figure 1.31

DRIED TIMBER

Figure 1.32

water given off a(i) → timber shrinks a(ii)

water absorbed b(i) → timber swells b(ii)

Figure 1.33

(a)   (b)

(c)   *Figure 1.35*   (d)

(y)

(x)

Figure 1.36

painting, varnishing or french polishing, etc. Not only does timber decrease or increase in size when the atmospheric conditions change, but it also changes in shape. For instance, a flat dry board that absorbs water will change its shape according to how it has been cut from the log. Figures 1.34 show three boards and what would happen to their shapes if moisture was allowed to evaporate from them.

Figure 1.35 shows that when a board increases or decreases in size it moves mostly in the direction of the growth rings. There is also movement in the direction across the growth rings, but not as much as in the former case. What shapes would the boards at x and y assume when they dry? It is important to choose a board that is suitable for the intended purpose. Flooring boards, skirting boards, solid panels in doors, solid table tops, etc. should all be quarter sawn. Softwood boards required for beams, roof timbers, floor joists, etc. should be tangentially cut because they rely partly on the growth rings for their strength. It does not matter if a beam is not perfectly flat as long as it is strong enough for the work it has to do. Figure 1.37 shows a beam. Place the growth rings on its end for a strong beam.

It is necessary to allow for movement in joinery items even when quarter-sawn boards are used because movement in solid timber cannot be entirely avoided. Figures 1.38 and 1.39 show boards used for flooring purposes. Show in the blank spaces what would happen if they were to shrink.

Figure 1.40 is the end of a form box for concrete. Show the direction of the grain in the timbers that would provide a strong box.

Figure 1.41 shows two skirting boards. Show what would happen if the boards were to shrink.

Figures 1.42 and 1.43 show the the incorrect and correct methods for fixing solid boards, such as table tops, to the sub-framing below. Figure 1.42 shows that the top has been fixed with screws passing through the top into the framing, resulting in splits due to movement in the solid top. Allowance must be made for this movement, so buttons or small metal plates, which act in the same way, should be used as in figure 1.43. A groove is made in each of the rails of the sub-framing, which is secured to the solid top by means of buttons, on one end of which a lip is located, as shown in the drawing. This arrangement will allow movement in the top, but still keep it secured to the framing.

Solid panels in doors, too, can split if the planted mouldings around them are fixed in a careless manner. Figure 1.44 shows the wrong way of carrying out this type of work because mouldings have been fixed to the framing with nails. If they pass through the solid panels, they will restrict

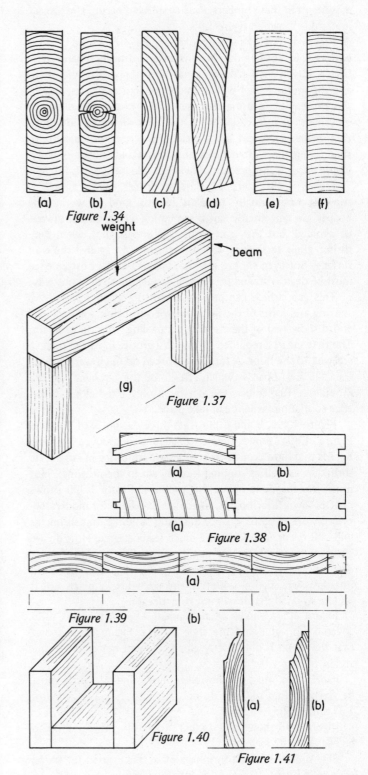

(a) (b) (c) (d) (e) (f)

Figure 1.34

weight

beam

(g)

Figure 1.37

(a) (b)

(a) (b)

Figure 1.38

(a)

(b)

Figure 1.39

Figure 1.40

(a) (b)

Figure 1.41

movement in these timbers, causing splits to occur. The correct method is shown in figure 1.45.

Figure 1.46 shows what could happen when a solid board is battened to keep it flat, for instance in drawing boards. The batten shown in the drawing has been screwed to the board and the method used will, as in the previous examples, restrict the movement, causing damage to the board. To allow for movement in such cases, the screw holes should be slotted, so that when movement takes place, the screws will be able to slide along the slotted holes and thus avoid splitting, which would occur if this precaution was not taken (figure 1.47).

Figure 1.48 refers to skirting boards, parts a and b showing what usually happens in this kind of work. The boards are tangentially sawn, something which cannot always be avoided, but they can be used as in b so that, when they shrink, their top edges will still remain tight against the wall surface. But even so, the gap that appears at the bottom edge must be dealt with and this can be done in more than one way.

This gap, which can be very unsightly, occurs because the skirting and joists of the floor below both shrink. Figure 1.48c and d show two of the methods for dealing with this problem. The first shows a moulded strip with a groove in its top surface screwed to the floor. A tongue is worked on the lower edges of the skirting boards which fit into the grooves of the mouldings. Remember, the skirting is only fixed along its top edge so that movement can take place.

Figure 1.49a, b and c illustrate three examples of flooring. Figure 1.49a shows simple tongued and grooved flooring boards that have been tangentially sawn, resulting in large-scale shrinkage as well as cupping (not shown in the drawing). Not much can be done about this problem. Figure 1.49b shows quarter-sawn floor boards. These are excellent for moderately priced work in better quality domestic buildings, but shrinkage will still occur, although to a much lesser degree. How do we get over this problem for quality jobs, such as dance floors? The answer is to use narrow-strip flooring that has been quarter sawn (figure 1.49c). Shrinkage will take place, but it will be so small that it will not be noticeable.

Figure 1.50a shows what happens when a tenon is fully covered with glue and the style shrinks. Figure 1.50b shows that the tenon is only partly glued, allowing movement in the style.

Panels, too, must be allowed to move, and mouldings must be fixed so that the pins do not pass into the panels (figures 1.51 and 1.52).

Figure 1.53 shows how timber shrinks at a mitre — this can be overcome by scribing.

Figure 1.54 shows a shrinkage plate that is used for fixing wide solid boards (figure 1.55) into base framing.

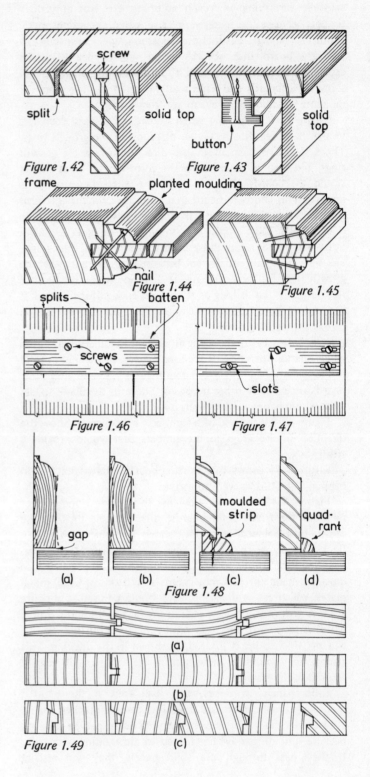

Figure 1.42

Figure 1.43

Figure 1.44

Figure 1.45

Figure 1.46

Figure 1.47

Figure 1.48

Figure 1.49

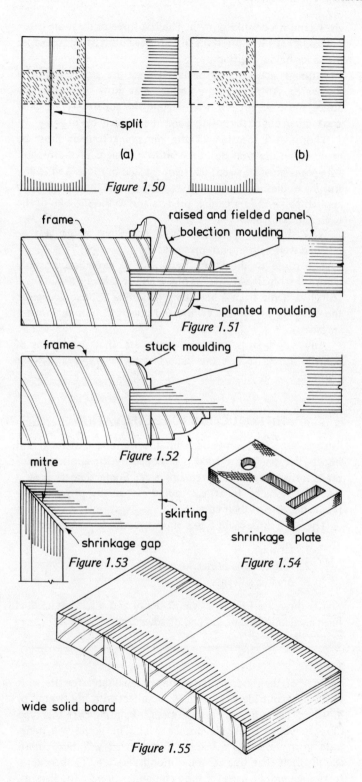

split

(a)   (b)

Figure 1.50

frame

raised and fielded panel
bolection moulding

planted moulding

Figure 1.51

frame   stuck moulding

Figure 1.52

mitre

skirting

shrinkage gap

Figure 1.53   shrinkage plate

Figure 1.54

wide solid board

Figure 1.55

	Yes	No
Is it always necessary to dry boards before they can be used for any purpose?	Yes	No
Is the water contained in the cell cavities known as the equilibrium moisture content?	Yes	No
Can there be any movement in timber all the time the cell walls are saturated?	Yes	No
Do quarter-sawn boards increase in size when they absorb moisture?	Yes	No
Are tangentially sawn boards more suitable for joinery purposes?	Yes	No
Is the greatest movement in timber in the direction of the growth rings?	Yes	No

COMMON CAUSES OF DECAY

Unless timber is installed and treated correctly, it can decay. Some forms of decay are present in the standing tree, but once the tree is felled and the timber dried these forms usually cease to exist.

Dry timbers placed in dry positions, are usually safe from attack, but if the site conditions change, the safety of the timber may be jeopardised.

Many timbers are naturally resistant to decay but others are more easily attacked. Sapwood is more likely to be attacked than heartwood because it contains more sugars and starches which provide food for the attackers. If there is any doubt at all whether or not a risk is being taken by placing a timber in a certain position, the timber should be treated with a preservative. This action — if done efficiently — has the effect of poisoning the food in the wood cells. Timber in contact with the ground is always liable to be attacked by fungus.

If timber is placed in a position where insufficient ventilation is present, such as a suspended ground floor, it can also be attacked by fungus. If timber is allowed to maintain a moisture content of more than 20 per cent, there is also a risk of fungus attack.

Some parts of Britain are danger areas as far as insect and fungus attacks are concerned and any timber used in these areas should be treated with a preservative.

Timber should never be placed in positions where there is moisture and lack of daylight because under these conditions fungus attack is usually just a matter of time. It should be remembered that an attack of the dry-rot fungus, once it has started will spread even if the conditions that caused the attack are removed.

Some causes of attacks by fungi are

(1)   timbers built into brickwork or masonry;

(2)   bad construction in ground floors;

(3)   ....

(4)   ....

(5)   ....

Fill in the blank spaces with other reasons why you think fungi attack wood.

DRY ROT

Dry rot is a fungus named *Merulius lachrymans*, or the weeping fungus, so called because it requires moisture to survive, but once it has begun to attack timber, it is capable of producing its own life-giving moisture.

Dry rot attacks timbers that have been allowed to become wet under conditions that enable the fungus to exist. These conditions include, in addition to the necessary amount of water

(i)   food in the timber — found mostly in the sapwood;
(ii)   a warm temperature;
(iii) lack of ventilation.

If softwood timber, containing more than 20 per cent of its dry weight of water, is placed in the conditions listed above, dry rot will attack it sooner or later; hence great care should be taken when placing timbers in suspect positions, such as in suspended ground floors.

To avoid dry-rot attack, air bricks must be placed around the walls of the building at such a level that the area underneath the floor is well ventilated. Sleeper walls must be built with openings between the bricks (honeycombing) to encourage the air to pass over the surfaces of the timbers. Damp-proof courses must be placed under all plates to which joists are fixed in addition, of course, to damp-proof courses in the main walls.

Provided that these steps are carried out properly, dry rot should never attack the timbers in that floor. But supposing an attack of the fungus has been discovered, what are the signs of dry rot in timbers and what must be done to eradicate it?

The signs of an attack of dry rot include a musty smell; cracks appearing across the width of the floorboards, skirting boards and architraves to doorways; white strands looking like cotton wool, called *mycelium* and millions of red spores looking like dust that are produced by the fruiting body, that gives a mushroom-like growth. The last three of these are often not apparent until the floor boards have been lifted to expose the space below the floor.

Ruthless action must be taken once the attack has been discovered. All parts of the timbers that show signs of fungus attack must be cut out well beyond the apparently attacked areas, taken out of the building and immediately burnt.

Thorough inspection of the remaining timbers must be made to ensure that no others show any signs of the fungus. All spores must be swept up, removed and burnt as well as any fruiting bodies. A hot liquid preservative must then be liberally applied to all the remaining timbers and to the surfaces of the walls and concrete.

New timbers, to replace those taken out, must also be brushed well with the hot preservative.

The cause of the attack must also be remedied, possibly before the repair work takes place, and an added precaution is to run a flame from a blowlamp or similar appliance over all the surfaces of the brickwork and concrete (not the timber surfaces!).

Any floorboards, skirting boards, etc. that show signs of damage should receive the same treatment as the underfloor timbers.

INTRODUCTION TO PRESERVATION

Timber, especially sapwood, contains the food that fungi and insects live on. If the food is poisoned by the application of preservatives the timber remains safe. Some timbers have a natural resistance to attack, but these usually prove uneconomic because of their cost.

There are three main types of preservative

1.   tar oils;
2.   water-borne preservatives;
3.   organic solvents.

All three are excellent against decay and insect attack and have particular advantages and disadvantages.

Tar oils

Because of their odour, these are more suitable for use with timbers for outside work that is in contact with the ground or in water. They do not corrode metals. Painting over this type of preservative is usually unsuccessful. The liquid will penetrate into plasterwork. Timber just treated will burn more readily than that treated some months before. Timbers thus treated cannot be used for food containers or near food stores.

Water-borne preservatives

These give good penetration into the wood. Usually, they do not smell and can be painted over when dried. They do not stain plaster work; therefore they are non-creeping. They do not make the wood flammable and do not corrode metals. They are suitable for internal and external use. Some preservatives of this kind can be used for food containers without any risk of tainting the food.

Organic solvents

This group of preservatives can be painted over when the solvent has evaporated. They can be used internally and externally, do not stain plasterwork, are non-creeping and do not corrode metals. They have good penetration properties.

Some of the solvents are inflammable and they must therefore be stored and used carefully. Some are unsuitable for food containers because their odour would taint the food. Also, they are not a danger to plant life and may be used for seed boxes.

To allow a preservative to give good penetration, the timber should be seasoned to remove moisture which would normally prevent the preservative from entering.

If the timber is to be cut or shaped, this should be done before the preservation is commenced, because if deep penetration is not obtained, shaping or sawing could expose unpreserved parts of the timber, thus allowing a fungus or pest attack.

APPLICATION OF PRESERVATIVES

The application of preservatives can be divided into two groups (i) non-pressure; (ii) pressure.

Non-pressure

(i) *Brushing*. The liquid is brushed on. Of very little value. Hardly any penetration (figure 1.56).

(ii) *Spraying*. Similar to brushing — has little value (figure 1.57).

(iii) *Dipping*. In-and-out method. Little better than the previous two. Slightly better penetration possible (figure 1.58).

(iv) *Steeping*. Timber left in the liquid for a short time. Reasonably good penetration depending on the type of wood (figure 1.59).

(v) *Hot-and-Cold method* (figure 1.60). Good penetration — much better than any other non-pressure method.

Two tanks are required, one with cold liquid and the other equipped to bring the liquid almost to boiling point. The timbers are placed in the hot liquid which will force the air out; this will be apparent by bubbles rising to the surface. When the bubbles stop, the timber is removed and placed in the cold tank where cold liquid will be sucked into the timber to occupy spaces vacated by the air. Much the best method: 100 per cent penetration can be obtained (figure 1.61).

Pressure (figures 1.62 and 1.63)

Full-Cell method. The timber is placed in a vacuum chamber and the vacuum is applied. The chamber is filled with preservative and the vacuum released. Liquid is sucked into the timber with almost full penetration. Cell cavities as well as walls are filled.

Empty Cell method. A second vacuum is applied, sucking out the liquid in the cavities, which is returned to the storage tanks. This can prove more economic than the full-cell method.

MOISTURE MOVEMENT

Principles of capillarity and surface tension

Surface tension. A liquid consists of millions of molecules, each of which is attracted to all those surrounding it. The molecules on the surface are only attracted sideways and downwards — not upwards. Therefore, the molecules within the liquid are in a state of equilibrium, but those on the surface are subjected to a constant pull downwards (and sideways at the interface with the containing vessel). This is seen if a glass of water is tipped slightly sideways so that the water is on the lip of the glass. As a result of a further slight tipping, the water will appear slightly above the lip of the glass. If a spot of water is allowed to spill on to a flat polished surface, it will appear in the form of a bead (see figure 1.64).

It is possible to overcome this attraction, or *surface tension*, as it is called, if the glass is tipped at a slightly greater angle when the water will spill over the side. If more water is allowed to spill on to the bead of water, it will spread over the surface once the surface tension has been overcome.

Surface tension can also be demonstrated with a soapy water solution. A clay pipe can be used with the soapy water to 'blow bubbles' — a favourite pastime for young children. Soap bubbles are held together and prevented from bursting by surface tension.

Make sketches to illustrate at least two more experiments that can be carried out to show the surface tension of a liquid.

PRESERVATION

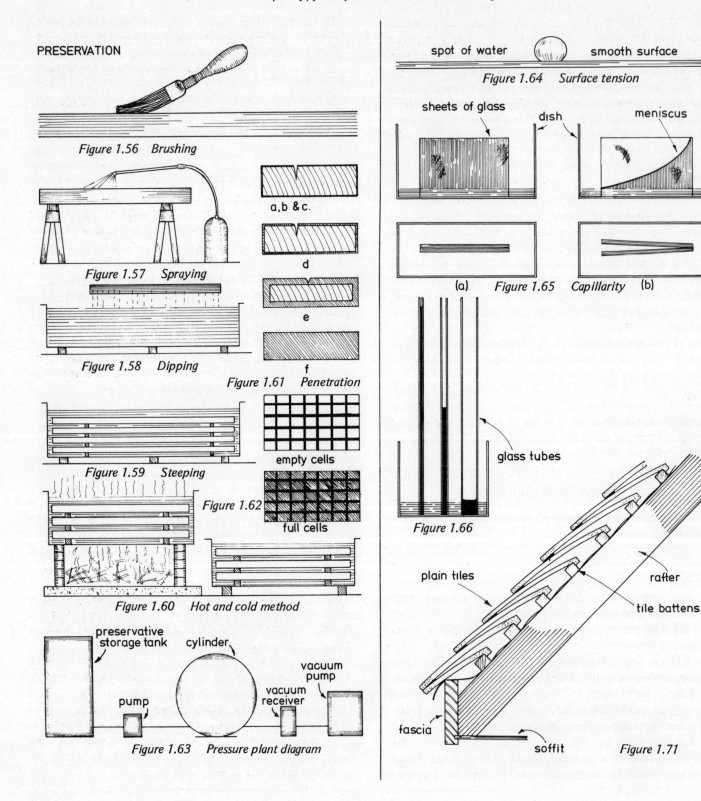

Figure 1.56   Brushing

Figure 1.57   Spraying

Figure 1.58   Dipping

Figure 1.59   Steeping

Figure 1.60   Hot and cold method

preservative storage tank

cylinder

vacuum pump

pump

vacuum receiver

Figure 1.63   Pressure plant diagram

a, b & c.

d

e

f

Figure 1.61   Penetration

empty cells

Figure 1.62

full cells

spot of water   smooth surface

Figure 1.64   Surface tension

sheets of glass   dish   meniscus

(a)   Figure 1.65   Capillarity   (b)

glass tubes

Figure 1.66

plain tiles   rafter

tile battens

fascia   soffit   Figure 1.71

Capillarity. Surface tension can also be seen to be present when two flat pieces of glass are held together in a dish of water. The surface tension will cause the water to be sucked up between the pieces of glass (see figure 1.65a). If the pieces of glass are separated slightly at one of their edges, it will be seen that the water between the glass will drop towards the water in the dish where the glass pieces have been separated. The curve which is formed by the surface tension of the water is called the meniscus (see figure 1.65b).

This phenomenon of water being sucked up between two close surfaces, can also be demonstrated with tubes of different diameter. The smaller the inside diameter of the tube, the higher the water will be drawn towards its top end (figure 1.66). For instance, the water in a tube of 5 mm inside diameter will be drawn upwards about 5 mm, whereas in a tube of 1 mm inside diameter the water will be drawn up to a height of about 30 mm. This ability of the water to travel upwards between two close surfaces or through narrow tubes is called capillarity. Widening the distance between the surfaces or enlarging the inside diameter of the tube causes the capillary action to be reduced.

Position and function of anti-capillary grooves, water bars and throatings

Water is essential in promoting the growth of a tree; it travels upwards from the ground to the leaves where it combines with carbon dioxide (photosynthesis) to yield food for the tree. The cells through which it travels are in the shape of very small tubes, whether they are tracheids (see page 16) in softwoods or vessels in hardwoods. Surface tension in the liquid probably contributes to this movement. This is another instance of capillarity.

In buildings there are many positions where capillarity can take place, thus causing damage, unless steps are taken to prevent this from happening. For instance, we must always place a damp-proof course under all carpentry timbers in the ground floors of buildings, because the pores in the brickwork act as capillary tubes allowing the passage of water. Wet timber in ground floors will eventually lead to fungus attack. Surface concrete of a building should also have a waterproof membrane sandwiched in its thickness because of its porous nature.

Joinery items, such as doors, windows, and French casements, can also be the cause of penetration of moisture into a building when they are badly designed.

External doors and door frames, especially at cill level are a common source of worry. Look at figures 1.67 and 1.68 and see how moisture penetration can be prevented by taking adequate precautions.

These illustrations show how water penetration can be overcome – overhanging cill with drip groove, groove for water bar on lower edge, water bar to fit up against edge of door and weather strip with drip groove fixed to front edge of door.

Figure 1.69 shows the cill and bottom rail to a casement window and also the head and top rail. Notice that anti-capillary grooves have been placed in the frame rebates and also on the casement bottom rail. No groove has been worked in the top rail of the casement since this would encourage water to collect in it. It has been replaced with an additional groove in the head of the frame.

Figure 1.70 shows how the water running off the surface of a flat roof can be prevented from reaching the timbers in the roof. A strip of wood has been screwed along the top edge of the facia or gutter board so that the felt covering the roof can be formed into a drip, well away from the woodwork.

Another roofing job, which does not affect people in the timber trades directly but which does give a good example of overcoming capillarity, is shown in figure 1.71. This is a tiling example and explains the camber in plain tiles. If they were flat, their surfaces would be close enough for water to be drawn up between them and this would eventually find its way into the roof timbers, possibly resulting in dry rot.

HARDWOODS AND SOFTWOODS

Hardwoods usually have broad leaves compared with the leaves of softwood trees. The latter are referred to as coniferous because they produce their seeds in cones and are exposed when they are ready to fall to the ground. The seeds of hardwoods are enclosed in a case, such as the chestnut and walnut.

Most softwoods are evergreen and hardwoods are usually deciduous, that is they shed their leaves at the end of the growing season. There are exceptions in each case, such as holly which is a hardwood and also evergreen.

Wood consists of many cells which run in the direction of the axis of the trunk, the one exception being the rays or horizontal parenchyma cells, which store surplus food.

During the growing season (during spring and summer in temperate zones) the tree produces a layer of new wood cells below the cambium. These are classed as 'springwood' and 'summerwood' cells. New bark cells are also produced by the cambium, but on the outside of the trunk.

Figure 1.72 shows the principal cells of hardwood trees.

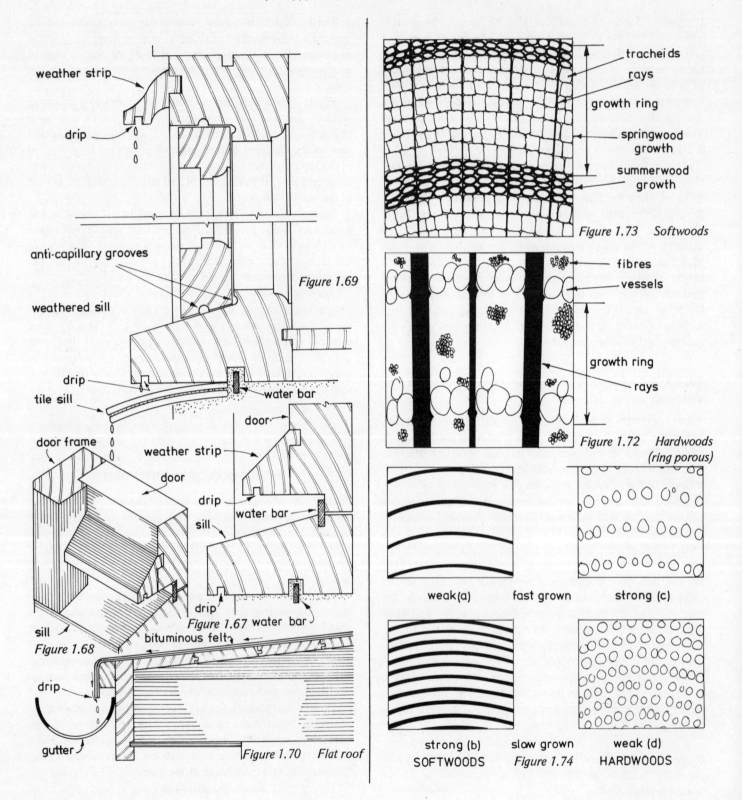

weather strip

drip

anti-capillary grooves

weathered sill

Figure 1.69

drip

tile sill

water bar

door frame

door

weather strip

door

drip

water bar

sill

drip

sill

Figure 1.68

Figure 1.67 water bar

bituminous felt

drip

gutter

Figure 1.70   Flat roof

tracheids

rays

growth ring

springwood growth

summerwood growth

Figure 1.73   Softwoods

fibres

vessels

growth ring

rays

Figure 1.72   Hardwoods (ring porous)

weak (a)   fast grown   strong (c)

strong (b)   slow grown   weak (d)

SOFTWOODS   Figure 1.74   HARDWOODS

These are vessels, fibres and parenchyma cells (rays). The fibres are the cells that give the strength to hardwoods.

The summerwood tracheids in softwoods are thick walled and give strength to the softwoods (figure 1.73). The thin walled tracheids in softwoods and the vessels in hardwoods, which are produced during the spring, are the sap-conducting cells.

Fast grown softwoods are considerably weaker than slow grown softwoods because the former obtain their strength from the summerwood growths of the tracheids, which have thick walls. Fast grown hardwoods are strong because these trees obtain their strength from the fibres spaced between the rows of vessels (figure 1.74).

SELECTION OF TIMBER

The selection of timber for a particular purpose is governed by several considerations, namely fitness for the purpose, cost, availability of supplies, costs of labour and machines to prepare and shape the timber.

For instance, if a general purpose timber is requi;ed for joinery and carpentry work, European redwood (yellow deal) would be an excellent timber to select. It can be used for almost any purpose in a domestic building; its cost is reasonable, various qualities, from joinery to carpentry grades, can be obtained fairly easily — most timber merchants hold adequate stocks — it can be worked well with hand and machine tools without blunting cutters and does not cause any trouble in the assembly of work. It can be glued fairly easily with any type of adhesive and can easily be painted or varnished.

Timber for good-class joinery purposes should be seasoned to the required moisture content and be free from defects, such as large or dead knots, splits and shakes. Preferably, it should be quarter sawn to keep movement to a minimum and the moisture content should suit the conditions in which it will be fixed.

Carpentry timbers should be strong and should be tangentially sawn, especially if they are to be used for joists or roof timbers. They should be seasoned down to a moisture content of 12—15 per cent. Large and dead knots should be avoided if strength is important and splits should also be avoided if possible.

General-purpose timber for joinery and carpentry work can be of a lower grade than those mentioned above, but very large and dead knots should be avoided.

Timber for rough work, such as concrete formwork, can be of low grade, but adequately supported where necessary.

Identification by inspection

Most craftsmen identify common timbers by their appearance. Oak, elm, beech, European redwood (red or yellow deal) and Douglas fir are usually very easy to identify. Other timbers are more difficult and other senses must be brought into action.

Variation in the colours of the heartwood and sapwood will sometimes lead to identification.

Other examples where the senses help in identification are:
Texture: whether coarse (elm), medium (mahogany, walnut) or fine (box, birch).
Surface: whether dull (teak) or lustrous (maple).
Feel: some timbers are cold (hornbeam), others are warm (gaboon), some feel oily or greasy (teak).
Odour: many timbers have a distinct odour (teak, cedar).
Weight: some are very light (balsa), others fairly light (obeche), medium weight timbers include European redwood. Heavy timbers include European oak, and *lignum vitae* is an example of very heavy timber.
Hardness: some timbers can be characterised by their hardness.

The length of splinters, and even the colour of wood ash is sometimes, although very rarely, a means of identification.

If the above means are not conclusive enough for identification, it will be necessary to resort to a hand lens (magnification x8 or x10). This is usually large enough to identify certain known features.

The end of the timber should be carefully trimmed with a very sharp instrument, such as a razor blade, before attempting identification with a lens. The lens must be held as near to the eye as possible and the specimen brought towards the lens until it is in focus.

When trying to identify softwood timbers conclusively, it is very often necessary to use a microscope because of their very minute structure.

Sources of supply

At this stage in the course it will only be necessary to deal with the more common timbers used by the construction industry.
Softwoods. The most popular softwoods used today are European redwood (red or yellow deal) and whitewood. The better grades are used for joinery and the more inferior grade for carpentry work, such as formwork. Although a native of Britain and often known as Scots Pine, European redwood is produced and imported from Sweden, Finland and Russia, as is whitewood. Lengths vary up to a little over 5 m, although longer lengths are obtainable at greater cost. Widths up to 150 mm are easily obtainable; timbers up to 200—250 mm are

less readily available and are therefore expensive. Loads or parcels of softwoods usually made up of hemlock, Douglas fir, spruce and Western Red cedar come from Canada. Fairly large lengths, especially of Douglas fir, are obtainable, as are slightly greater widths than that of European timbers. Hemlock is more of a carpentry timber (roofs, floor joists). Douglas fir is used for joinery and structural work and Western Red cedar is a very durable timber which can be used for exterior purposes.

A large quantity of Parana pine is used in Britain for joinery purposes, such as staircases, and comes mainly from Brazil. Greater widths than those previously mentioned are readily available up to 350 mm.

Hardwoods. Many hardwood timbers are in common use; in contrast to softwoods, they come from a variety of countries. There are of course, several home-grown timbers, such as English oak, elm and ash, which have many uses in the home market, but many hardwood timbers are imported from Africa, whose forests were virtually untapped until the Second World War.

African timbers include afrormosia, agba, idigbo, iroko, African mahogany, makory, mansonia, obeche, utile and sapele. Other hardwoods in common use in Britain are beech (Europe), jarrah (Australia), American mahogany (Belize), mahogany (Central America), meranti (Malaysia), oak (Japan, Europe), padauk, teak (Burma), ramin (Borneo), rosewood (India), sycamore (Europe) and walnut (Europe).

Hardwood logs are usually converted into boards of various widths.

When ordering a quantity of softwood boards it is possible to ask for boards of any required width and thickness provided they conform to stock sizes.

With hardwoods, however, thicknesses can be asked for, but the boards will most likely be of random width.

TIMBER SIZES

[British Standard (BS) 4471: 1969 and BX 4471, Part II, 1971]

For economic reasons timber work for joinery or carpentry purposes should be designed with timber stock sizes in mind.

When a rod for a joinery job is prepared, an allowance must be made for the preparation of the timber by machine — at least 5 mm off the width and thicknesses of a board is usual.

In expressing the dimension of a piece of timber, the order in which they should be expressed should be as follows:

length x width x thickness

When placing an order for timber, it should be remembered that when the width of the boards increases so does the price by a much greater proportion.

Softwoods lengths are sold by the metre run and prices are usually quoted for 100 m run. The thicknesses and widths of required boards must be given in millimetres (mm).

Some prepared boarding will be sold by the square metre (sq m or m²).

Lengths of softwood boards are sold in stock size, lengths starting at 1.8 m rising in 0.3 m increments to 6.3 m.

Hardwoods may be sold in the following thicknesses (in mm) 19, 25, 32, 38, 50, 63, 75, 100 and 125, and then upwards in 25 mm stages to whatever maximum it is possible to supply any particular hardwood.

Sheet materials will be sold in sheet sizes, all dimensions being given in millimetres, for instance

2440 mm x 1220 mm x 19 mm

When designing or setting out work, the foregoing stock sizes should always be kept in mind so that wastage of material will be cut to a minimum.

For instance, when setting out a rod for a door, the stiles and top rail could be prepared from 100 x 50 mm stock, the bottom rail from 200 x 50 mm and intermediate rails from 75 x 50 mm. As allowances have to be made for planing, the sizes of these pieces would be shown on the rod as being, say, stiles and top rail 95 x 45 mm, bottom rail 195 x 45 mm, and intermediate rails 70 x 45 mm.

Supposing the sizes on the rod showed the top rail and stiles as being 100 x 50 mm, the next stock size upwards from these dimensions would have to be used, namely, 125 x 63 mm, resulting in a very high waste.

What sizes of timber would you use for the following components?

Component	Sawn sizes		Finished sizes	
	Width	Thickness	Width	Thickness
Hardwood window cill	125	75		
Middle rail of door			145	32
Stile of casement			95	70
Head of door frame	75	50		

ADHESIVES

The selection of the correct adhesive, where these are to be used, is important for two reasons:

(i) economically it is unsound to use an expensive adhesive where a cheaper one is capable of doing the work required;

(ii) it is uneconomic to select an adhesive if it is not capable of doing the job required.

Some adhesives are expensive, others much cheaper, so it is necessary to know those that are available to the wood trades and also to know what they are designed to do.

Scotch glue

The most common adhesive is Scotch glue which is made from the bones or hides of animals. It has gone out of favour in recent years because of its limitations and the time required for its preparation. It can be obtained in slab, pellet and jelly form and is prepared by heating. To make it usable, water is often added to the melted glue. It can only be used in warm conditions and it must be used quickly because of its fast cooling, which renders it less efficient. It is not a glue to be recommended because it cannot be used on site, like almost all the others.

Casein adhesive

This is bought in powder form to which water is mixed to give a usable creamy consistency. It is derived from sour milk and can be used in the workshop as well as on the site and under low-temperature conditions.

After mixing it should be left to stand for about half an hour when it will be ready for use. It has a working life of up to seven hours. It is not particularly durable in moist conditions and it can also be attacked by micro-organisms. It is used in all forms of interior joinery, furniture and interior-grade plywood. Its disadvantage is that it stains some timbers.

Synthetic resin adhesives

(i) Urea formaldehyde. This adhesive will withstand very adverse conditions up to several years. It is supplied in syrup form with a liquid hardener, or it can be obtained in powder form (which contains the resin and hardener) and mixed with water. It is used for joinery, furniture and plywood.
(ii) Phenol formaldehyde. This has very good properties. In particular, it is very durable in adverse conditions. It is purchased as a resin with a separate liquid hardener. It is used for exterior plywood and joinery and timber engineering purposes.
(iii) Resorcinol formaldehyde. This adhesive is suitable under all types of conditions. It is purchased as a liquid to which is added a powder hardener, which can also be obtained as a

liquid. It is used for all types of external work, including marine and harbour installations.
(iv) Polyvinyl acetate. This adhesive has poor resistance to damp conditions, but is an excellent glue for all furniture and internal joinery items. It is sold as a white creamy liquid.
(v) Contact and impact adhesives. This type of adhesive is not particularly resistant to dampness and is inflammable; hence care must be taken when using it. It is sold as a thick creamy liquid. Both surfaces must be covered with the glue and allowed to dry, which takes about 15 minutes. They are then brought together and pressure applied. It is very useful for gluing laminated plastic sheets to wood surfaces and plywood sheets to walls.

TYPES OF MANUFACTURED BOARDS

Plywood comprises an odd number of veneers the direction of each running in the opposite direction to those with which it is in contact (figures 1.75a and b). This makes plywood superior to solid timber as far as strength is concerned because it is strong in all directions, whereas solid timber is comparatively weak in the direction at right angles to the grain. This strength makes plywood useful for carpentry purposes, such as form-work for concrete. The construction of plywood enables it to resist movement due to moisture absorbtion and also makes it impossible to split, enabling nails to be driven in without pilot holes first being drilled. There are various grades of plywood and the correct grade should always be used for a specific job.

This grading applies to the type of adhesive used.

Int. This is the interior grade and, as the name implies, should only be used internally and in dry conditions.
M.R. This grade is moisture resistant and moderately weather resistant and should only be exposed to the elements for a limited period.
B.R. This means boil resistant and this grade has good resistance to exposure to the elements, but fails under very long exposure.
W.B.P. Weather and boil proof. This grade has a high resistance to weather conditions, cold and boiling water, steam, dry heat and micro-organisms.

Laminboard, blockboard and battenboard

These materials are similar to plywood; they are built up in layers, but, in contrast to plywood, the two outer layers are veneers and the centre core comprises strips of solid timber (see figures 1.75c, d, e and f). In laminboard, these strips are

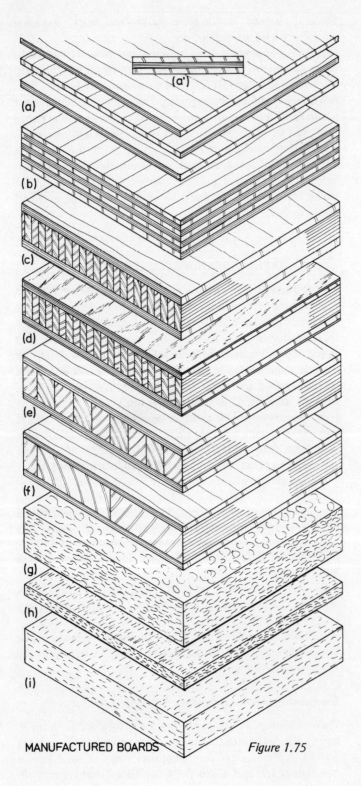

up to 7 mm wide. In blockboard, they are up to 25 mm wide and the strips in battenboard can be very much wider.

The direction of the grain in the outer veneers is at right angles to that of the strips forming the core. Sometimes there are two veneers on each side of the core. In this case the direction of grain will be as seen in Figure 1.76d.

These boards can be used for a variety of purposes, such as flooring, kitchen fitments, furniture, cabinets and built-in fitments.

Chipboard

This board is often named resin-bonded chipboard and as the name implies, comprises wood chips bonded together into a sheet material by a synthetic resin, see figure 1.75g.

Several grades are available for flooring and roof decking. Sheets can also be obtained with wood face veneers and with laminated plastics.

Hardboard (figure 1.75h)

This is a fibre board composed of a mixture of paper and finely ground wood chips, brought to pulp form by mixing with water, and subjected to pressures between platterns.

Fibre insulating-board (figure 1.75i)

This is similar to hardboard, but subjected to much less pressure.

2. TOOLS

To become as proficient as a craftsman, an apprentice carpenter and joiner must collect a set of tools of good quality and to save a few pence on each tool is a mistake. Good quality tools will always do what they were designed to do and, if used correctly and expertly they will perform each operation quickly and efficiently.

As a result of practice, the young craftsman must be able to use each of his tools properly; he must be able to recognise and know the name of each tool, and also know what each is capable of doing. He must also keep them in a good state of repair.

SETTING-OUT AND MARKING-OUT TOOLS

The first job in the production of an item is usually to *set out* the work. This means drawing sections through the job, the details of which are obtained from the designer's drawing, so that the person who is to prepare the material can see all the necessary details. Examples of setting out will be given below.

The tools required for setting out — which is done on a sheet of paper or plywood, or a narrow width of board — are similar to those described in the section on geometry (chapter 14). These comprise a rule, pencils, large set squares, a metric scale rule (for scaling the designer's drawing) a T-square, drawing pins, rubber, compasses, etc.

Marking-out tools are required for putting various marks on pieces of timber that will, when assembled, produce the required item.

The *try square* (Figure 2.1) is used for marking lines on a piece of timber by means of a pencil or by using a marking knife (figure 2.2). It has a stock which is held firmly against the edge of the board and a blade along which the line is marked. The blade and stock form an angle of 90°, but when marking or measuring a 90° angle with a try square, it must be remembered that only the inside edge of the stock should be used.

Care should be taken not to drop the square because this will tend to loosen the blade from the stock. It is common practice to test the squareness of this tool when new and periodically throughout its life. If found to be out of square, a file, carefully used on the blade, can restore it to its correct squareness.

The *sliding bevel* (figure 2.3) is similar to the try square, except that the blade and the stock can be adjusted to any required angle. The blade and the stock are held together with a screw that can be either released by a screwdriver or a quick-release nut. It is useful for marking splayed shoulders to tenons, etc. The blade has a slot along which the stock can slide; this can be useful for marking left-hand and right-hand bevels of the same number of degrees. Remember, too, that angle x° and angle y° equal 180 degrees.

The *mitre square* comprises a blade and a stock and is a useful tool for marking 45° angles. Both sides of the stock can be used for marking the bevels (see figure 2.4).

The *marking gauge* (figure 2.5) is used for marking out lines along the length of a piece of timber in the direction of the grain and also across its ends. It consists of a rod and a sliding fence. A metal spur is fixed at one end of the rod and the fence can be adjusted to any position along its length and secured by a boxwood screw. Two brass strips are sometimes let into the face of the fence nearest to the spur in order to prevent wear. The spur should be kept sharp by using a file. Some craftsmen drill a hole in the rod at the opposite end to the spur. This hole should be large enough so that a pencil may be inserted with some effort so that the gauge can be used for placing a pencil line on the wood instead of a cut line. This is necessary when marking chamfers and bevels along the length of a piece of timber. Marking with a cut line would create difficulties because the line would be difficult to remove. A saw cut should be made between the pencil hole and the end of the rod to give a little spring to the wood that will enable the pencil to be gripped in its hole. Figure 2.6 shows how the marking gauge is used.

The *mortice gauge* (figure 2.7) is similar to the marking gauge

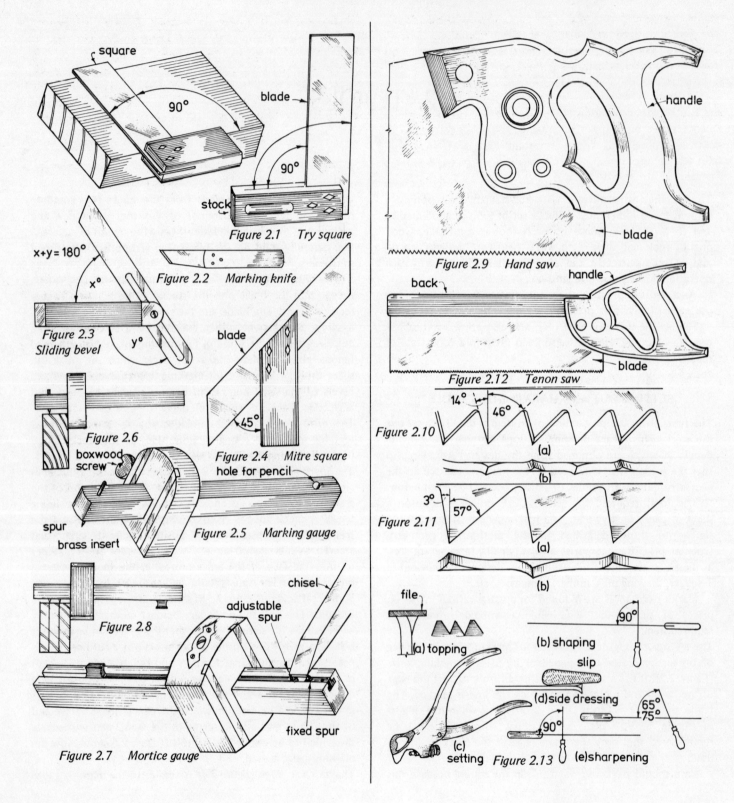

square

90°

Figure 2.1   Try square

blade

90°

stock

x+y = 180°

x°

y°

Figure 2.3
Sliding bevel

Figure 2.2   Marking knife

blade

45°

Figure 2.4   Mitre square

Figure 2.6

boxwood
screw

spur

brass insert

hole for pencil

Figure 2.5   Marking gauge

Figure 2.8

chisel

adjustable
spur

fixed spur

Figure 2.7   Mortice gauge

handle

blade

Figure 2.9   Hand saw

back

handle

blade

Figure 2.12   Tenon saw

14°   46°

Figure 2.10

(a)

(b)

3°   57°

Figure 2.11

(a)

(b)

file

(a) topping

(b) shaping

90°

slip

(d) side dressing

(c)
setting   *Figure 2.13*   (e) sharpening

90°

65°
75°

but has two spurs at one end of the rod: the spur farthest from the fence is fixed and the other can be adjusted to any required distance from the first. This enables the craftsman to mark two parallel cut lines along the length and also across the ends of timbers.

The fence is secured in position by a screw which also assists in holding the adjustable spur in its set position. The mortice gauge is used for marking the positions of tenons, mortices, grooves, etc. The spurs should first be adjusted to the width of the cutter, as shown in the drawing; the fence is then placed into its position and secured. Figure 2.8 shows the use of a mortice gauge for marking the width of a tenon. Again, the spurs should be kept sharp with a file.

Fill in the spaces in the chart below

Tools	Operations
(i)	Marking shoulders to tenons
(ii)	
Mortice gauge	
	Testing that the end of a piece of timber is square
Mitre square	
	Marking the edges of a rebate along a length of timber
	Marking the edges of a chamfer along a length of timber

SAWS

Hand Saws. There are two kinds of hand saw — those used for cutting along the direction of the grain in the board and those for cutting across the grain. They differ mainly in the shape of the teeth, but there are other differences, such as the number of teeth per 25 mm and the length of the saws. Figure 2.9 shows the handle end of a hand saw.

Crosscut saws are used for cutting across, or at right angles to the grain but also for general purposes. The largest is 650 mm long with 5—7 teeth per 25 mm. The shortest of these is called a panel saw, 500 mm long with 8—10 teeth per 25 mm (figure 2.10).

Rip saws are used for cutting down the length of a piece of timber along the direction of the grain. This saw is usually about 700 mm long and has 3—4 teeth per 25 mm. Rip saw teeth are shown in figure 2.11.

The tenon saw is another type of crosscut saw. It has a metal strip, either of steel or brass, running along its top edge that acts as a reinforcement strip and enables the saw blade to remain straight. It is used for cutting shoulders to tenons, recesses in boards for shelves and many similar jobs (figure 2.12) (300—350 mm long, 12 teeth per 25 mm).

Saws are maintained by keeping the teeth sharp and in good shape, chiefly by the use of files. After a saw has been sharpened and set a few times, the teeth may become irregular and to restore them to their original state the following steps must be taken

(1) *Topping* — A flat file is drawn across the teeth to bring the tops into alignment, (figure 2.13a).

(2) The teeth are then shaped by using a three-cornered file until they regain their original shape, (figure 2.13b). The file is held at right angles to the saw.

(3) The teeth are then given a set which means that, with the aid of a saw set, the tip of every other tooth is bent over to one side of the saw and the remaining teeth are bent over in the other direction, as shown in figure 2.13c.

(4) Next, the teeth are given a side dressing with an oilstone slip (figure 2.13d). This involves rubbing the slip along the sides of the teeth on both sides of the saw to bring the edges into line.

(5) Lastly, a three-cornered file is used for sharpening the teeth. For cross-cut saws, the file is held at $65°—75°$ to the saw blade; the direction of the file strokes must be towards the saw handle, pointing slightly upwards. For rip-saw teeth, the file should be held at $90°$ to the saw blade and in a horizontal direction.

Saws for cutting curves. Other types of saw are used for cutting curves, which requires a much narrower saw than those already mentioned.

The bow saw (figure 2.14) consists of a wooden frame and a narrow strip of saw blade that is held firmly between the lower ends of the side members. The saw is held taut with a strong chord and a wooden peg placed across the top of the frame. The inset drawing shows how this saw is used for cutting curves in fairly thick materials such as boards and blockboard.

The coping saw (figure 2.15) consists of a metal U-shaped frame with a thin saw blade stretched across its lower part. The saw is tensioned by turning the handle in one direction and the tension is released by turning it in the opposite direction. The saw anchors can be turned in their sockets so that the saw teeth can be made to face downwards, upwards or sideways, as desired. The blade is usually placed in the frame so that cutting is done by the backward strokes. This tool may be used for cutting thin materials, such as plywood.

Figure 2.16 shows a keyhole saw, which consists of a

narrow blade and a handle through which the blade can pass. The blade is held in position by one or two screws. This kind of saw is useful for cutting keyholes for locks and for any other small job for which other saws are not suitable.

Figure 2.17 illustrates a compass saw with three separate blades. It may be used for cutting holes in floors, partitions, etc.

PLANES AND CHISELS

Planes

Metal planes are much more popular to-day than wooden planes which are now considered to be old-fashioned. The weight of metal planes is an advantage when they are in use, but it is a decided disadvantage when they have to be carried from job to job. Figure 2.18 illustrates a *metal jack plane* which is approximately 380 mm long. Its main use is to prepare timber from the sawn state since its length enables the craftsman to produce a reasonably flat piece of timber.

The metal-smoothing plane (figure 2.19) used for producing a good finish to a flat surface, is constructed similarly to the jack plane and a glance at the cross-section through the smoothing plane shows that the handle and front knob are secured to the metal body by screws. The cutting iron is inclined at approximately 45° in the plane and is much thinner than the irons found in wooden planes. The lower end of the back or cap iron (which is secured to the cutting iron by a screw) should be about 1—1.5 mm from the cutting edge; its function is to break the wood shavings off at very close intervals to avoid the wood splitting along the length of the cut. The cap iron and cutting iron are securely clamped in position by a lever cap. Figure 2.20 shows a cutting iron and a cap iron assembled ready for placing in the plane.

Plane maintenance consists chiefly of keeping the cutting iron ground and sharpened correctly and the lower surface of the body clean and free from scratches, etc. After long use and many sharpenings it will be necessary to regrind the iron. This should be done carefully to produce an angle of approximately 25°; the iron should then be sharpened on an oil stone to give an angle of 30° (figure 2.21).

Figure 2.22 shows a *metal rebate plane* for cutting rebates. It has a cutting iron that can be placed in either of two positions. The depth of cut can be adjusted by turning a circular nut near the top of the cutting iron. The width of the rebate can also be controlled by adjusting the fence which is secured to two metal rods by means of screws. A metal spur and a depth gauge located on the far side of the plane enable a rebate to be cut to any desired dimensions without having to

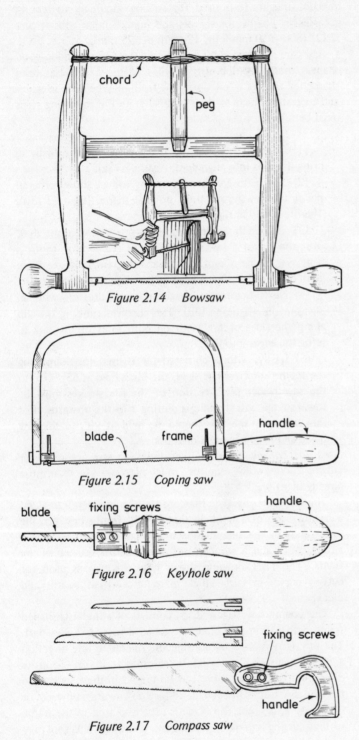

Figure 2.14   Bowsaw

Figure 2.15   Coping saw

Figure 2.16   Keyhole saw

Figure 2.17   Compass saw

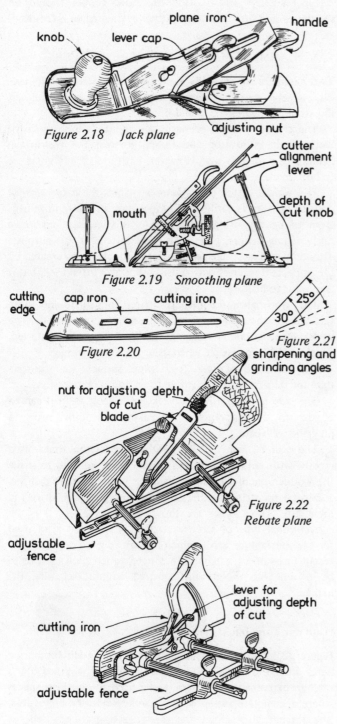

Figure 2.18   Jack plane

Figure 2.19   Smoothing plane

Figure 2.20

Figure 2.21 sharpening and grinding angles

Figure 2.22 Rebate plane

Figure 2.23   Plough plane

mark out the amount of wood to be removed prior to cutting the rebate.

The plough plane shown in figure 2.23 is used for cutting grooves. A lever is situated behind the iron to adjust the depth of cut. The adjustable fence enables the groove to be cut in the correct position. Various widths of cutters are supplied with the plane.

Wood chisels

Various types of chisels in common use in shops where work is still done by hand methods are illustrated in figure 2.24(a)–(f).

The *firmer chisel* (a) is a general purpose cutting tool that can be used for heavy work as well as for better-quality carpentry work. It may be obtained with beech handles, but most joiners prefer the harder boxwood or plastic handles. It is used for paring shoulders to tenons (figure 2.25) and for removing waste from grooves across the grain, etc.

Bevel edged chisels (b and c) may be used for similar jobs as the firmer chisel, but are usually reserved for joinery work.

The chisels illustrated comprise two types of gouge – the inside ground (d) and the outside ground (e) gouge. The former is used for paring work with a concave surface and the latter for work with a convex surface (figure 2.26).

The mortice chisel (f) is probably least used nowadays. As the name implies, it is used for cutting mortices, but since it is not an economic proposition to cut mortices by hand, this chisel is rapidly becoming outmoded.

Chisels must be kept sharp if they are to give good service. After sharpening them several times, they have to be re-ground – preferably on a wet stone although, for quickness, it is often done on an emery wheel, which could prove detrimental to the steel if care is not taken. The grinding angle of a chisel is similar to that used for plane irons – 25°. Sharpening is done with an oilstone on to which is poured a small amount of thin oil (figure 2.27). The chisel should be held at an angle of approximately 30°, but many joiners hold their chisels much lower, at approximately 25°, which is equal to the grinding angle, the reason being that the lower the sharpening angle, the keener the cutting edge, which will also keep its sharpness longer. But, this makes the edge more prone to damage.

When the sharpening has been completed, the burr on the cutting edge has to be removed by holding the flat surface of the chisel on the surface of the oilstone and rotating the chisel. It may also be necessary to go through the sharpening and removal of burr actions alternately to ensure its complete removal (figure 2.28).

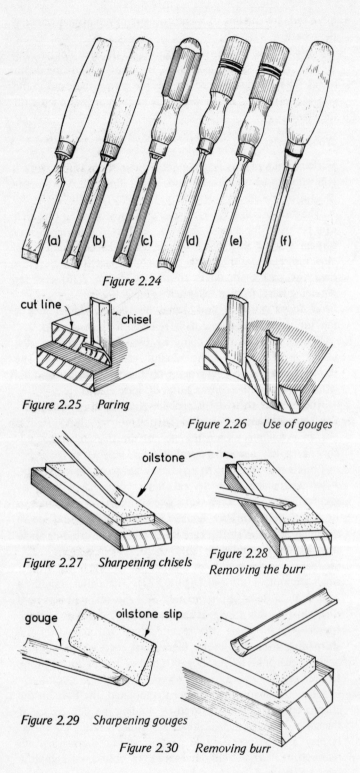

Figure 2.24

Figure 2.25   Paring

Figure 2.26   Use of gouges

Figure 2.27   Sharpening chisels

Figure 2.28   Removing the burr

Figure 2.29   Sharpening gouges

Figure 2.30   Removing burr

Figures 2.29 and 2.30 show how gouges should be sharpened and how the burr on their cutting edges is removed.

HAMMERS, MALLETS AND SCREWDRIVERS

Two hammers are generally found in a carpenter's and joiner's kit, namely, the *claw hammer* and the *Warrington hammer*, illustrated in figures 2.31a and b.

The claw hammer is primarily a carpenter's tool for heavy work, such as roofing and floors, whereas the Warrington hammer is a joiner's tool. However, both tools are of great use to both men.

The weight of the claw hammer enables the carpenter not only to drive nails easily into timber, but also to remove nails from timber by using the claw. As this leverage requires a fairly strong handle, hickory is most suited for this purpose. This timber is also able to absorb the shock waves created by the impacts it receives during use. Ash is also often used, but it is inferior to hickory.

The Warrington hammer is lighter in weight and more suitable for the small type of nail used in joinery work. The wedge shape at one end enables small panel pins to be started, which may be impossible when using the claw hammer.

The *ball pane hammer*, (c) is more suitable for engineers than for joiners, but it can prove to be useful on occasions.

The *club hammer* (d) is a bricklayer's tool; again it can be of use to the carpenter when raking out joints prior to plugging walls, etc.

The mallet (figure 2.32) is another impact tool that is used mostly with chisels. Hammers should never be used to strike the wooden handles of chisels because of the possible damage.

Most carpenters and joiners have a variety of screwdrivers in their kits. Three types are shown in figure 2.33 — a is the conventional type of screwdriver; b is the Phillips type, used for the special-type screw which has gained great popularity in recent years; c is a ratchet screwdriver, which allows screws to be driven into wood and removed without releasing the handle.

Hand brace and bits

Figures 2.34 and 2.35 show a handbrace — used for boring holes in wood — and three types of bits. The brace has a ratchet that enables the tool to be used in confined spaces where a complete sweep of the handle would be impossible. The ratchet also allows the reverse action to be used for removing bits in awkward positions.

The twist bit shown in 2.35a is probably the most common

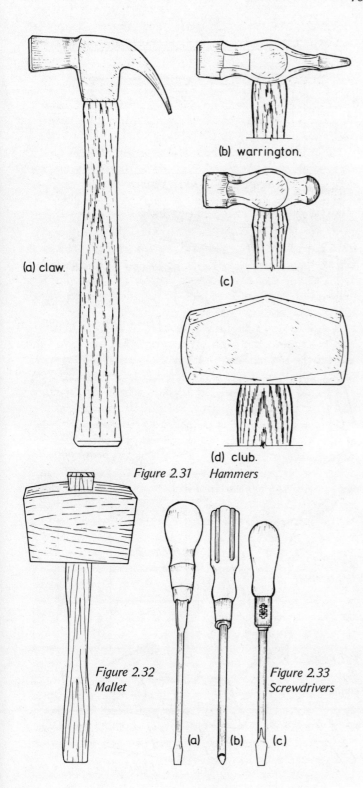

(a) claw.

(b) warrington.

(c)

(d) club.

Figure 2.31　Hammers

Figure 2.32
Mallet

Figure 2.33
Screwdrivers

(a)　(b)　(c)

type of bit used in the brace and is usually supplied in assorted sizes for holes from 3 mm up to 25 mm diameter. Any hole larger than 25 mm diameter is made with an expansion bit or with the coping or bow saw. Figure 2.35b illustrates the centre bit used for cutting holes in thin materials, such as plywood and figure 2.35c shows a countersink bit for countersinking holes for screws.

Figure 2.36a is another boring tool called a wheel brace that is more useful for boring holes for nails and screws. The type of bit used in the wheel brace is called a morse drill (figure 2.36b).

Figure 2.37 shows a pair of dividers for drawing curves on timber and for other work, such as scribing timber to irregular surfaces.

Figure 2.38 shows a bradawl — useful for marking the position of holes to be drilled and for making holes in materials for nails, etc.

Figure 2.39 illustrates a pair of trammel points connected by a batten or beam. This tool is used for setting and marking out work, especially where large circles are required. It is possible to replace one of the metal points with a pencil when required.

Pincers (figure 2.40) are used for removing nails from timber. When used on good class work, a piece of plywood or similar material should be placed between the work and the pincers to avoid damage to the surfaces.

Figure 2.41 shows a scraper that is used for cleaning up joinery work to produce a good smooth surface free from marks that would be left if glasspaper were used. To render a scraper capable of cleaning up a surface efficiently, its longer edges must first be filed flat and then a burr created on all corners by using a burnishing tool. The sharpening process has to be repeated periodically.

A glasspaper block that is used with any required grade of paper for the preparation of surfaces is illustrated in figure 2.42.

Figure 2.43 shows a nail punch that can be obtained in various sizes, from a pin punch for panel pins to one that can be used for larger nails.

Two dovetail templets for marking out dovetail joints are shown in figure 2.44.

Figure 2.45 shows a metric tape rule which can be obtained in several lengths.

WORKSHOP ACCESSORIES

A *joiners bench* (figure 2.46) can be obtained in many sizes and should be constructed in such a way that it provides a

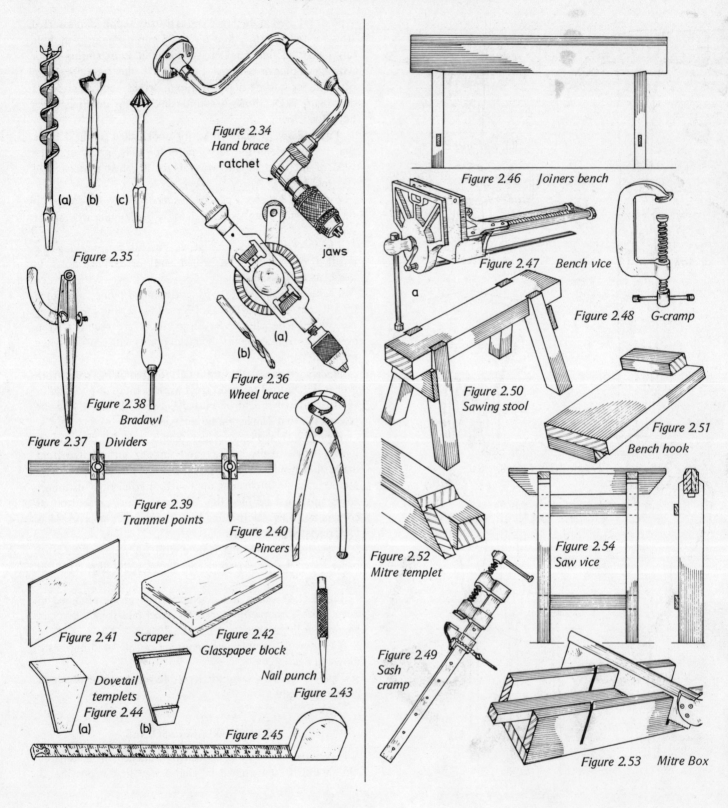

(a)   (b)   (c)

Figure 2.35

Figure 2.34
Hand brace
ratchet

jaws

(b)   (a)

Figure 2.36
Wheel brace

Figure 2.38
Bradawl

Figure 2.37   Dividers

Figure 2.39
Trammel points

Figure 2.40
Pincers

Figure 2.41   Scraper

Figure 2.42
Glasspaper block

Nail punch

Figure 2.43

Dovetail
templets
Figure 2.44
(a)   (b)

Figure 2.45

Figure 2.46   Joiners bench

Figure 2.47   Bench vice

a

Figure 2.48   G-cramp

Figure 2.50
Sawing stool

Figure 2.51
Bench hook

Figure 2.52
Mitre templet

Figure 2.54
Saw vice

Figure 2.49
Sash
cramp

Figure 2.53   Mitre Box

good solid surface on which a large variety of work can be done, ranging from the construction of simple joints to the manufacture and assembly of large pieces of carpentry or joinery.

A bench vice (figure 2.47) is an essential part of the bench — it is used for holding timber to be cut, shaped and prepared and to assist in the assembly of work.

The G-cramp (figure 2.48) is used for clamping timber to the bench or to other surfaces, for clamping several pieces of timber together, etc.

The sash cramp, (figure 2.49) is used in a similar way to the G-cramp and also for other purposes, such as cramping up frames during assembly.

The sawing stool (figure 2.50) is often used in a pair and is most useful for resting boards that are to be sawn. It is also useful for assembly work, etc.

The bench hook (figure 2.51) is used at the edge of the bench for resting smaller pieces of timber when crosscutting.

Accurate mitres can be obtained using a mitre templet (figure 2.52) — a very useful tool when mouldings on the framework edges have to be mitred. The templet is placed over the moulding in the correct position; the mitre can be cut by using a chisel to pare away the moulding, resting the back surface of the chisel on the bevelled portion of the templet.

The mitre box (figure 2.53) is another mitre-cutting tool. Two saw cuts are placed across the width of the box to coincide with the bevels required; the timber is placed in the correct position in the box, and the mitre is cut with a tenon or hand saw.

The saw vice (figure 2.54) is used for clamping hand or tenon saws during the sharpening process.

SITE ACCESSORIES

Several tools are used on the site that assist builders to carry out their work efficiently. The carpenter not only uses some of these tools, but he is often asked to manufacture some of them.

The first of these is a straightedge (figure 2.55). It is used by many craftsmen, such as plasterers, carpenters, joiners, bricklayers and concreters. The example shown has only one perfectly straight edge, but this tool is often made with two parallel edges. With the help of a spirit level (figure 2.56) the concreter will use the straightedge to check that the tops of pegs are level (figure 2.57). Plasterers use straightedges when plastering walls and screeding floors. Joiners use straightedges for checking levels to which joinery has to be fixed, also for checking the straightness of a piece of timber (figure 2.58).

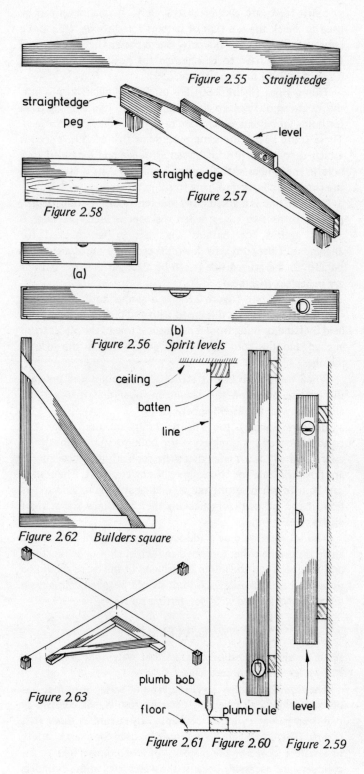

Figure 2.55   Straightedge

Figure 2.57

Figure 2.58

(a)

(b)

Figure 2.56   Spirit levels

Figure 2.62   Builders square

Figure 2.63

Figure 2.61   Figure 2.60   Figure 2.59

Spirit levels are also used separately. A small level can be used to check the position of battens for shelving, etc., and a larger level is used, for example, where battens have been fixed to a wall and have to be checked for position before sheet material is fixed to them (figure 2.59).

Plumb rules (figure 2.60) are used for similar purposes as the larger spirit level. In this case, a plumb rule is being used for lining up battens which have been fixed to the wall surface. These could be for the same purpose as figure 2.59. A cord is attached to the centre of the straightedge and extended to a hole in the timber. At this point, a metal weight is attached to the cord and adjusted to hang freely in the hole.

A gauge line is marked down the centre of the straightedge, parallel to its two edges; when the tool is used, one edge is placed against the battens that are to be checked for alignment. If the cord runs down the centre of the straightedge parallel to the gauged line it can be assumed that the battens are in perfect alignment.

The plumb bob (figure 2.61) is a similar tool, but in this case the straightedge is dispensed with and the top of the cord is held by hand or hung from a nail against one of the pieces to be aligned and the cord is extended downwards to the second member.

When the plumb bob is stationary, its point will indicate the precise point on the second member that is in vertical alignment with the top member.

Builders squares too (figure 2.62) are useful for the construction of right angles on the building site, although the apprentice will learn later that more sophisticated instruments are now available for checking right angles on site. The square can be used when setting out a building and figure 2.63 shows how it can be used for checking that two lines are at right angles to each other.

The square should be made accurately; the joint at the right angle should be either morticed and tenoned or open morticed and tenoned, and the joints at each end of the brace should be dovetailed and halved. Each joint should be glued with a resin adhesive and secured with non-ferrous screws.

WATER LEVELS

Water levels are based on the fact that water will always find its own level if it is unrestricted.

The *Aqualev* (figure 2.64) is a type of water level that has been developed to give very accurate results — it consists of two transparent cylinders connected by a rubber tube. It is comparatively inexpensive and may be used for a large variety of levelling jobs. For the majority of jobs no markings on the cylinders are necessary because the water level in the cylinders

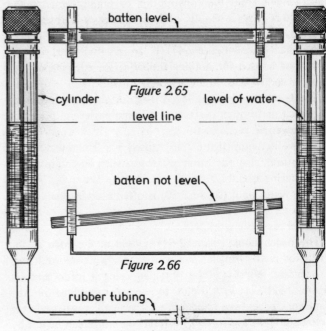

Figure 2.65

Figure 2.66

Figure 2.64   Water level

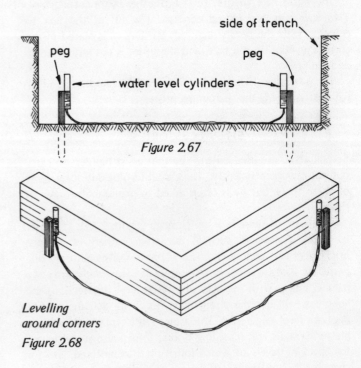

Figure 2.67

Levelling around corners
Figure 2.68

is used to check the level of the objects. However, when the levels of two items have to be compared, it will be necessary to have some means of comparison. This can be done by clipping a graduated plate behind each cylinder to the difference between the two water levels.

The plates are also used if pegs have to be placed in the ground to give a fall to the concrete bed for pipes, etc. The top of each cylinder has a specially constructed cap; when the level is not in use, this cap should be in its tightened up position, otherwise the water in the level will be lost. A plunger valve is fixed below each cap, which closes the hole at the bottom of the cylinder leading into the rubber tubing. The closing of this hole will prevent air from entering the tube, which would result in an incorrect reading due to the presence of an air lock. The caps are loosened after the two cylinders have been positioned to check a level, thus releasing the water and allowing it to find its level. When the water level has come to rest, the two cylinders should be moved slowly so that the water level in the cylinder at the starting point is level with the mark being used for levelling — a datum mark, or similar indication. The water level in the second cylinder will be identical with that at the datum point.

When the water level is in use, no kinks should be allowed to occur in the rubber tubing and when levelling has been completed, the caps at the tops of the cylinders should be tightened to prevent loss of water.

Figures 2.65 and 2.66 show the water level in use. Figure 2.65 shows a level line and figure 2.66 shows that a fixed batten is not in a level position.

Figure 2.67 shows pegs in a trench, the tops being in line with the water levels in the tubes.

Figure 2.68 shows that the level can be used for positioning pegs round a corner.

(a) A metal shoulder plane may be used for the following

(i) Finishing the shoulders to tenons ....

(ii) ....

(iii) ....

(b) A plough plane may be used for the following

(i) ....

(ii) ....

(iii) ....

(c) A spokeshave may be used for

(i) ....

(ii) ....

(iii) ....

3. JOINTS

BASIC WOODWORKING JOINTS

Woodworking joints can be divided into three groups

    (i) lengthening
    (ii) widthing
    (iii) angle joints

Lengthening joints are used when available timbers prove to be too short for the job in hand.

Laminated beams are an example and figure 3.1 shows a beam built up from a number of short lengths of board with the joints distributed evenly throughout. These laminations are glued together and held in a series of clamps until the glue has set. Laminating timbers in this way will enable the carpenter or joiner to produce a strong length of timber to any required dimensions — in structural work, this method is used to produce timbers of any required shape as well as for straight work.

Figure 3.2 shows how these beams can be used: over an opening such as a garage doorway, and supported on built-up posts. The posts can be made to any dimensions; in rough work, such as timbers for supports, the pieces can be nailed securely together to form a large bulk of timber (figure 3.3).

Other types of lengthening joints can be seen in figs 3.4 and 3.5. Figure 3.4 shows a handrail bolted joint connecting two timbers lengthwise; this type of joint is used in joinery work. The two timbers are butt jointed, the hole for the bolt in each piece being carefully positioned by using a gauge. The holes should be drilled and small mortices made in the edges of the timbers so that the nuts to the bolt can be inserted. One of the nuts is round and can be tightened by using a punch and hammer. Figure 3.5 shows how the head of a curved frame is built up using curved laminations.

Widthing joints enable us to build up narrow widths of timber into wider boards. The most common of these joints is the butt joint (figure 3.6), which comprises two timbers planed square and straight on the two meeting edges and glued together to form a single board.

Figure 3.7 is a tongued and grooved joint consisting of a tongue worked on the meeting edge of one of the two pieces and a groove of similar dimensions on the other. If the joint is to be glued (as it would be for joinery purposes) the tongue should be slightly shorter than the depth of the groove to allow the joint to come up tight. Both pieces of timber are often grooved and a loose tongue of plywood is inserted. This joint is considered to be superior in strength to the butt joint if an additional gluing surface is required.

Since the Second World War, great strides have been made in the development of adhesives for woodworking that are now completely reliable with regard to strength provided that they are used for the purposes for which they were intended. Before modern glues were available there were many variations in joints used for increasing the width of timber — these variations are not necessary now. They included slot screwed joints and others, which, if made at present, would make the work uneconomical. The butt joint described earlier will be strong enough for most purposes.

Figure 3.8 shows another tongued and grooved joint used in secret fixing to floor boards in high quality work.

Figure 3.9 shows the tongued and grooved joint found in built up panel work, for example in the ledged and braced door (p. 99).

This material is termed *matchboarding* and in addition to the tongues and grooves, beads and V-joints are also included in the preparation of the boards.

Another type of board used for panel work is called shiplap boarding (figure 3.10). It is often seen on the elevations of buildings and is used as covering material for timber buildings and site offices. The joint can be termed tongued and grooved with the variation seen in the drawings.

Figures 3.11 and 3.12 show two ways of ensuring the flatness of solid timbers which have been made wider. Figure 3.11 shows a rebated batten held against the board by means of lipped buttons which are screwed to the board. This method allows the board to move, while keeping it flat. Figure 3.12 shows another method of holding a board flat

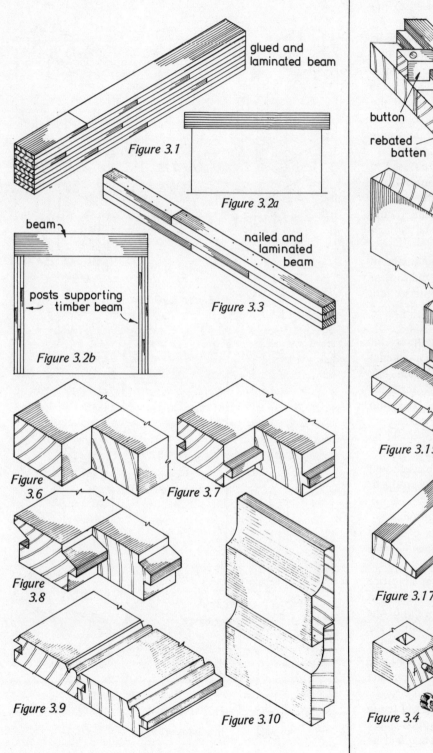

glued and laminated beam

Figure 3.1

Figure 3.2a

beam

nailed and laminated beam

Figure 3.3

posts supporting timber beam

Figure 3.2b

Figure 3.6

Figure 3.7

Figure 3.8

Figure 3.9

Figure 3.10

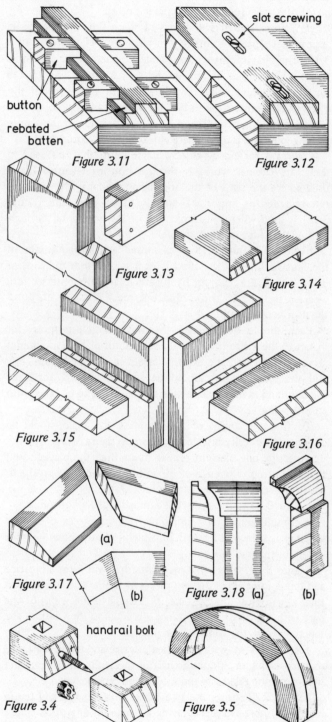

slot screwing

button

rebated batten

Figure 3.11

Figure 3.12

Figure 3.13

Figure 3.14

Figure 3.15

Figure 3.16

(a)

(b)

Figure 3.17

Figure 3.18 (a)

(b)

handrail bolt

Figure 3.4

Figure 3.5

while allowing it to move. The battens are screwed to the board, the holes for the screws being slotted.

Angle joints Isometric drawings of some simple angle joints appear in chapter 14; others are illustrated in figures 3.13–3.18. The first of these, the simple notched joint, shown in figure 3.13, is used in carcase and similar work. The joint is simply glued and nailed or screwed with the heads of the screws well countersunk so that the holes can be filled.

The mitred halving (figure 3.14) is a variation of the simple halving joint and is used where a neat finish is required.

Figures 3.15 and 3.16 show angle joints that are used in shelf and cabinet work. A through housing (figure 3.15) is used where the sight of the housing on the face of the work is not regarded as important, and the stopped housing (figure 3.16) is used where this projection of the horizontal through to the front edge is not desirable.

Figures 3.17 and 3.18 show mitred and scribed joints. In the illustration of the mitred joint it is seen that the ends of both pieces are cut to fit together at their intersection, whereas figure 3.18 shows that one piece is cut to fit round the profile of the other.

Each should be used for the most suitable purpose; for instance, the mitre joint should be used for planted mouldings around panels and the external angles in skirting boards, etc. and the scribed joint should be used in internal angles of skirtings and in particular where shrinkage has to be taken into consideration.

To find the angles of a mitre joint, the angle should be drawn and carefully bisected as shown in figure 3.17b.

To scribe one piece of timber to another, the piece should first be mitred. The edge of the mitre will show the profile to which the scribe is to be cut (figure 3.17a).

Figures 3.19–3.23 show various mortice and tenon joints.

A simple joint for joining two square pieces of timber together is shown in figure 3.19, which indicates how the joint should be marked out.

Figure 3.20 shows the two parts that will form a mortice and tenon joint when the two pieces of timber have grooves on their edges. Note that distance y is equal to the width of the part with the tenon and distance x is equal to the width of the tenon and also the width of the mortice.

Figure 3.21 shows a haunched mortice and tenon joint, the mortice taking up the inside half of the width of the rail and the haunching taking up the second and outside half.

Figure 3.22 shows the two halves of a mortice and tenon joint, the morticed piece having a rebate on one of its edges. This means that one of the shoulders to the tenon will be longer than the other.

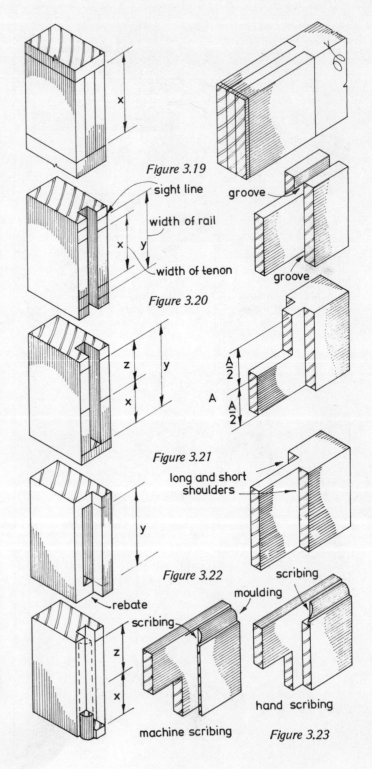

Figure 3.19

sight line

groove

width of rail

width of tenon

groove

Figure 3.20

Figure 3.21

long and short shoulders

Figure 3.22

scribing

moulding

rebate

scribing

hand scribing

machine scribing

Figure 3.23

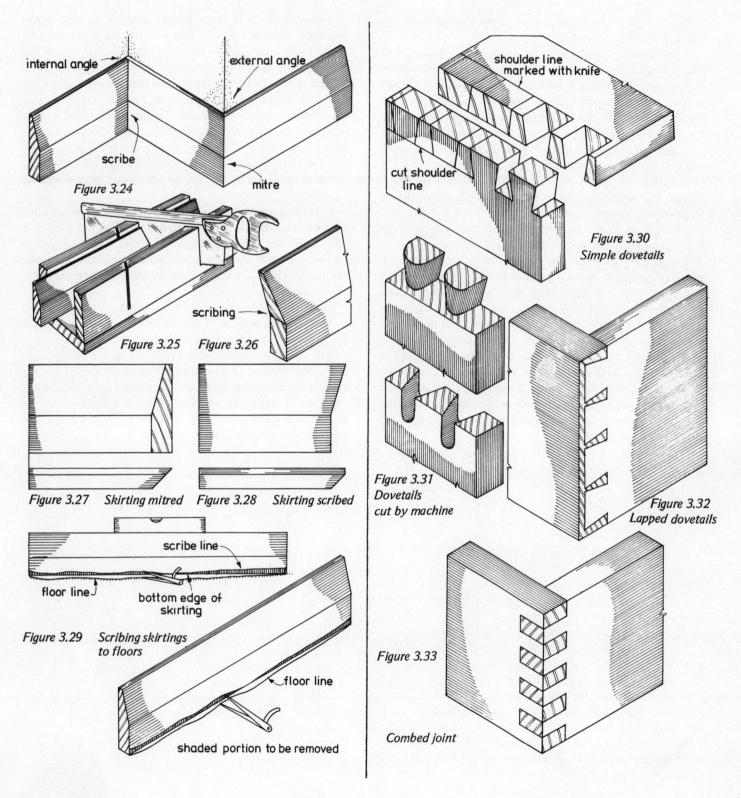

internal angle

external angle

scribe

mitre

Figure 3.24

scribing

Figure 3.25　　*Figure 3.26*

Figure 3.27　*Skirting mitred*　*Figure 3.28*　*Skirting scribed*

scribe line

floor line

bottom edge of skirting

Figure 3.29　*Scribing skirtings to floors*

floor line

shaded portion to be removed

shoulder line marked with knife

cut shoulder line

Figure 3.30 Simple dovetails

Figure 3.31 Dovetails cut by machine

Figure 3.32 Lapped dovetails

Figure 3.33

Combed joint

Figure 3.23 shows a mortice and tenon joint with mouldings that are to be scribed.

Where the joint is to be machine-scribed, the scribing will pass through the entire width of the material (see illustration in the centre). When the joint is hand-scribed only a small portion of the moulding is scribed into the shoulder, the remaining length of shoulder remaining square. In figure 3.23, the illustration on the left shows the morticed part of the joint. For machine-scribing, the moulding passes through to the end of the piece (shown by the broken lines) but in hand-scribed work, the length of the moulding is sufficient only to fit into the scribing on the other piece, the rest being removed, as also shown in this illustration.

Figure 3.24 shows two skirting joints, the internal angle being scribed and the external angle mitred.

Figure 3.25 shows how the mitred joint is prepared and the prepared scribing is shown in figure 3.26.

Figures 3.27 and 3.28 show plans and elevation of the last-named joints and scribing of a piece of skirting to an uneven floor is seen in figure 3.29. The skirting is first placed over the uneven surface and levelled with a spirit level. A pair of dividers are then set to the widest gap between skirting and floor and then with one point of the dividers set against the floor and the other point against the skirting, the dividers are used to mark the profile of the floor on the board surface. The part of the board below the scribing line must be removed so that the skirting may fit against the floor surface.

Figures 3.30–3.32 show various types of dovetail joints. In simple through dovetails (figure 3.30) the joints must be marked out accurately if they are to be cut by hand and shoulder lines should be cut with a knife in order to produce straight clean shoulders. The dovetails are marked with a dovetail templet and then squared over across the thickness of the material with a try-square. The waste material is then removed from between the dovetails when the pins can be marked on the other piece by placing the dovetails across its end and marking with a sharp pointed scribing tool. The pins can then be prepared and the two halves of the joint fitted together.

Machine dovetails (figure 3.31) are produced by using only a machine, for instance an individual dovetailing machine or a vertical spindle. The general opinion is that machine dovetails are not as neat as the hand-made dovetails, but provided that the machine is set correctly, they are as strong as those made by the joiner.

Figure 3.32 shows lapped dovetails that have been prepared by hand. This type of joint is used where strength is required in addition to a plain surface on the face of the work.

The combed joint (figure 3.33) is also a machine-made joint, but it may be produced by hand. It is used for the cheaper type of work, such as boxes, carcase work and cabinet work which is hidden from view. Although these joints are not as neat as the dovetailed joint, they can prove just as efficient provided that modern glues are used.

4. PORTABLE POWERED HAND TOOLS

Electrically operated hand tools are generally considered to be the tools of the carpenter and joiner — machinists do not often use them. They can be very dangerous if used incorrectly or carelessly and their potential danger must be recognised.

Many power tools have in recent years become available for 110 V supply, especially for work on building sites. They are much safer in use and a shock from this lower voltage would not prove fatal, which could be the case when operating on 240 V. Nevertheless, these lower-voltage tools must be treated correctly. In some workshops, tools are driven by a 50 V power supply. Some power tools can be obtained with double insulation, which means that it is impossible for an operative to receive a shock from the tool. Hence the manufacturers use two-core cables, the earth wire being unnecessary.

However, many portable tools are still driven by a 240 V power supply and need to be earthed. To prevent mistakes in the use of tools designed for different power supplies, it is usual to fit different types of plugs and sockets for each kind so that damage will not be done by connecting them to the wrong power supply. It must be remembered that neglect on the part of users of power tools may lead to very serious injury. It is essential to observe the safety precautions and to understand how the machine works; how it should be used, and its work capacity. The user should make certain that the tool is in good working order and that the correct power supply is available. Every power tool should be inspected for faults at regular intervals by an experienced person. If a fault occurs, the tool should be taken out of use immediately and returned to store. It is important to attach a note stating the reason why it has been returned.

The cables leading from the power source to the tool should also be inspected regularly and renewed in the case of damage or wear. When used on site, they can be damaged if traffic is allowed to pass over them. Kinks in the cable should be avoided since they can cause damage. Carrying a tool from one place to another, with the lead over the workman's shoulder and the tool hanging down his back can cause the leads to be separated from their connections (figure 4.1).

Never adjust a portable tool while it is plugged into the power supply — careless switching-on by a practical joker while adjustments are being made could cause severe injuries. Also, before inserting the plug into the socket after adjustments have been made, make sure that the 'on/off' switch on the tool is in the 'off' position. Never pull the plug out of its socket by pulling on the cable (figure 4.2). This too can detach the leads from their connections.

If a change in sound of a portable tool is noticed during use, switch the power off and have the tool inspected for faults.

Safety goggles should be worn in many cases, especially if abrasive materials are being used. Dust masks should be used too, especially when working with asbestos and other dust-producing materials.

Safety guards supplied with the machine should be used at all times. Fixing the trigger switch to the 'on' position to relieve the job of constantly applying pressure with the finger is not recommended, because if the tool should slip and come to rest against the operator's body, injuries would result because of his inability to release the switch to stop the machine.

The workpiece should be clamped on the bench or securely held to prevent if from moving during shaping.

The operator should concentrate his attention on the work he is doing and not allow anyone or anything to distract him.

Never place the tool on a bench or other surface before it has stopped — it may be damaged or may travel along the surface due to the rotary action of the motor and drop to the floor possibly injuring a bystander.

Cables should be kept well clear of the tool while it is in motion because this is another cause of damage to cables that could possibly result in the operator receiving a severe electric shock.

To safeguard himself further, the operator should wear protective clothing and never allow his tie or, for that matter, long hair, to get anywhere near the machine. If he has long hair, he should wear a hat of some sort; roll his sleeves up, and

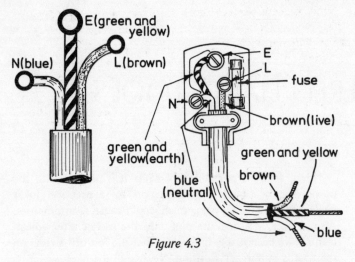

N(blue)   E(green and
             yellow)
           L(brown)

E
L
fuse
N
brown(live)
green and
yellow(earth)
green and yellow
brown
blue
(neutral)
blue

Figure 4.3

Figure 4.6

Figure 4.4

Figure 4.1

Figure 4.8

Figure 4.5

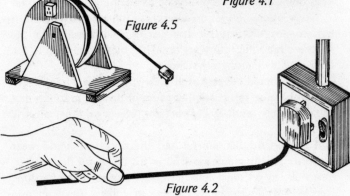

Figure 4.2

Figure 4.9

tuck his tie into his shirt opening — all these measures are designed to prevent accidents.

When portable-tool cables have to be connected to the tool or plug, it is important to know the colour code of the cable. It is as follows

live wire	....	brown lead
neutral wire	....	blue lead
earth wire	....	green and yellow stripes

Older machines will have the outdated wire colour coding, namely

live wire	....	red
neutral wire	....	black
earth wire	....	green

The portable tools to be covered in this stage of the course are the drill, the sander and the powered screwdriver.

Figure 4.3 shows the standard type of socket and plug for 240 V tools. It has three rectangular pins, the larger of the three being the earthing pin. Double insulated 240 V tools with twin cables can be connected to the plug, no wire being joined to the earth pin.

Figure 4.4 illustrates a 50 V plug and socket that may be placed overhead for convenient use at a joiner's bench; they are also used for tools with twin and 3-core cables, but care must be taken to join the wires from the tools to their correct leads.

Figure 4.5 shows an extension lead — a useful accessory when the power supply is at a distance from the workplace. All extension leads should be wound round a drum when not in use, otherwise kinking will occur resulting eventually in damage to the cable.

Figure 4.6 shows a portable power drill — probably the most frequently used tool in the entire range of power tools. It may be used for drilling pilot holes for screws and nails, for drilling holes in brickwork with the aid of a tipped drill and for drilling holes in metal.

In addition to the work just mentioned the larger type of power drill can be adapted for cutting mortices with a hollow chisel and auger, which are similar in construction to those which are used in the hollow chisel morticer, see page 71. In order to adapt it for morticing, a stand is required to which the drill is clamped (figure 4.7). This can save the carpenter much effort, but the power drill and stand is not such a precision tool as the morticing machine; however, it is a useful accessory on building sites where no machines are available.

Figure 4.8 shows the method of fixing a morse drill in the chuck of the machine.

Most modern portable drills have two speeds; the faster speed is used for drilling holes in wood, the slower speed for drilling holes in brickwork, metal and similar materials.

Usually the speed is changed merely by turning a switch on one side of the tool. This should be done before the machine is started.

Figure 4.9 shows a drill being used for drilling a hole in a piece of timber.

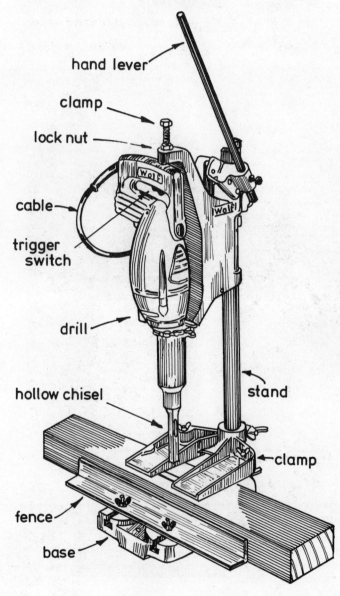

Figure 4.7

Mortising with a drill

Figure 4.10

Figure 4.13

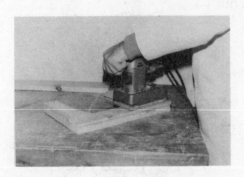

Figure 4.11

Figure 4.14

Figure 4.12

Figure 4.15

Figure 4.10 shows an orbital sander, so called because the pad or base to which the sandpaper is attached travels in a very small circle, the direction of travel being parallel to the surface of the pad. This tool is called a finishing sander because it is used for finishing the flat surfaces of joinery work.

Figure 4.11 shows the orbital sander in use. Only slight downward pressure is required for efficient operation but persons using the tool for the first time press down on to the timber much too hard — this results in the pad remaining stationary on the timber while the top of the machine rotates. Start the machine while it is not touching the timber and lower it onto the timber surface gently and then guide it backwards and forwards to obtain the required finish.

The piece of sandpaper will soon become worn and will have to be removed and replaced. To remove the paper a screwdriver is needed to turn the screw at each end of the pad; a new sheet can be inserted by reversing this procedure (figure 4.12).

The belt sander (figure 4.13) is used for large-scale work, such as the preparation of wide boards or the cleaning up of the surface of a block floor, etc. Figure 4.14 shows how the belt sander is used.

Figure 4.15 shows how a sandpaper belt can be removed from the sander before inserting a new one. On this machine which is made by the Wolf company, the belt is released by moving a small lever into the vertical position (as seen in the illustration); the belt can then be removed and a new one put in its place. The Wolf electric screwdriver in figure 4.16 is used where a large amount of repetition driving or removing of screws is required. Various sizes of bit are obtainable; they are replaced by grasping the bit, as shown in figure 4.17, and pulling it out of the chuck. The other bit is inserted into the chuck and pushed home. Figure 4.18 shows an electric screwdriver in use.

Figure 4.17

Figure 4.18

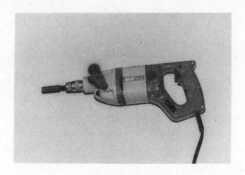

Figure 4.16

Figure 4.19

This tool has two speed settings that can be changed to suit the work in hand. The slower speed is used for driving screws in wood, the faster for screws in metal. Figure 4.19 shows how the speed can be changed by adjusting the button in the front of the body of the tool to the required speed. Pressure on the machine when applied on the screw will start the drive and releasing the pressure will stop the machine.

Fill in the spaces below to complete the chart

Portable tools and accessories	Operation(s)
(i) Screwdriver	
(ii) Screwdriver bit	
(i)	Holes for plugs in wall
(ii)	
(i)	
(ii)	
(iii)	Cutting mortices
(i) Orbital sander	
(ii) Fine grade glasspaper	
(i)	
(ii)	Cleaning up large board

5. WOODCUTTING MACHINERY

This section of the book covers only the basic woodcutting machines, as laid down in the City and Guilds syllabuses (Part I). Its aim is to enable the student to recognise each machine; to know how to ensure the maximum safety for the operator; to appreciate what the machine can do and how it operates and the requirements for the machines to run at their maximum efficiency.

Carpenters and joiners, too, must acquaint themselves with woodcutting machinery since it has now become un-economical to use the numerous manual methods that were practiced only a few years ago. A large part of the joiner's work will be the assembly of joinery items from components prepared in the machine-woodworking shop, but a thorough understanding of each other's craft will enable these two important crafts in the construction industry to turn out work in an efficient manner.

It is certainly not unknown for joiners in comparatively small builders' workshops to select materials, set out and mark out, prepare the components on the available machinery and assemble and finish the work without any help from other craftsmen. Hence, it is important that joiners as well as machinists should have a good understanding and knowledge of the various woodcutting machines.

The student must also have a thorough knowledge of the safety regulations in force for woodcutting machinery that form part of the Factories Act. The metric version of these has been published recently (the *Woodworking Machines Regulations, 1971*) and it is the duty of the employer as well as of the employee in every firm using woodcutting machinery to ensure that these regulations are carried out without fail.

The Woodworking Machines Regulations, 1971, which came into operation in 1971* (except Regulation No. 42), are divided into eight parts. Part I explains the interpretation and exemptions. Part II contains the general regulations regarding

*The final draft of these Regulations was published after this book went to press. The reader should acquaint himself with the minor differences from those printed here.

woodworking machines; Parts III to VII describe the regulations applicable for various machines and Part VIII covers miscellaneous items. (Extensive extracts from these regulations are reproduced below.)

It is necessary to point out that most woodworking machines are dangerous and that every operative must, for his own sake, know these regulations by heart and perform them to the letter. Many accidents are caused by boredom, lack of concentration and repetitious work. It is the duty of every operative to do everything possible to avoid accidents to himself and to others by keeping the machine guards correctly adjusted; he must report if a machine is not functioning efficiently; he must concentrate on his work and not attract another person's attention to himself, or, indeed, to allow another person to distract him while he is working at a machine.

The operative should never allow the area around his machine to become cluttered with ends of timber or other items (as laid down in the regulations) and spanners and tools should be removed from the machine before the current is switched on. Indeed, no adjustments must be made to a machine while it is running – the machine must be switched off and the isolator turned to the 'off' position. Safety aids must be used at all times if the work necessitates such aids.

THE WOODWORKING MACHINES REGULATIONS, 1971

Part II all woodworking machines – general

Provision and construction of guards

5. – (1) Without prejudice to the other provisions of these Regulations, the cutters on every woodworking machine shall be enclosed by a guard or guards to the greatest extent that is practicable having regard to the work being done thereat, unless the cutters are in such position as to be as safe to every person employed as they would be if so enclosed.

(2) All guards provided in pursuance of the foregoing

paragraph of this Regulation shall be of substantial construction.

Adjustment of machines and guards

6. No person shall make any adjustment to any part of a woodworking machine or to any guard thereon, while the cutters are in motion, except where the adjustment can be made without danger.

Use and maintenance of guards etc.

7. — (1) At all times while the cutters are in motion, the guards and devices required by these Regulations and all such safeguards as are mentioned in Regulation 8 shall be kept constantly in position and properly secured and adjusted except when, and to the extent to which, because of the nature of the work being done, the use of any such guard, device, or safeguard is rendered impracticable:

Provided that the said exception shall not apply to the use of any guard required by Regulations 18(2), 23 or 28.

(2) The said guards, devices, and safeguards, and all such appliances as are mentioned in Regulation 14(1)(*b*) shall be properly maintained.

Exception from obligations to provide guards etc.

8. Regulations 5, 16, 21, 22, 26, 28, 30, 31 and 36 shall not apply to any machine in respect of which other safeguards are provided which render the machine as safe as it would be if the provisions of those Regulations were complied with.

Machine controls

9. Every woodworking machine shall be provided with an efficient device or efficient devices for starting, and cutting off the power to, the machine and the control or controls of the device or devices shall be in such a position and of such design and construction as to be readily and conveniently operated by the person operating the machine.

Working space

10. There shall be provided around every woodworking machine, while the cutters are in motion, sufficient clear and unobstructed space to enable, in so far as is thereby practicable, the work being done at the machine to be done without risk of injury to persons employed.

Floors

11. The floor or surface of the ground around every woodworking machine shall be maintained in good and level condition and, as far as reasonably practicable, free from chips and other loose material and shall not be allowed to become slippery.

Temperature

12. — (1) Subject to the following provisions of this Regulation, effective provision shall be made for securing and maintaining a reasonable temperature in every room or other place (not in the open air) in which a woodworking machine is being worked.

(2) In that part of any room or other place (not in the open air) in which a woodworking machine is being worked, a temperature of less than 10 degrees Centigrade shall not be deemed at any time to be a reasonable temperature except where and in so far as the construction of the room and the necessities of the business carried on make it impracticable to maintain a temperature of 10 degrees Centigrade.

(3) Where it is impracticable for the aforesaid reasons to maintain a temperature of 10 degrees Centigrade in any such part of a room or place as aforesaid, there shall be provided to the extent that is reasonaly practicable, effective means of enabling persons working there to warm their hands.

Training

13. — (1) No person shall be employed on any kind of work at a woodworking machine unless:

(*a*) he has been sufficiently trained at machines of a class to which that machine belongs in the kind of work on which he is to be employed and

(*b*) he has been sufficiently instructed in accordance with paragraph (2) of this Regulation,

except where he works under the adequate supervision of a person who has a thorough knowledge and experience of the working of the machine.

(2) Every person, while being trained to work at a woodworking machine, shall be fully and carefully instructed as to the dangers arising in connection with such machine, the precautions to be observed, the requirements of these Regulations which apply and, in the case of a person being trained to operate a woodworking machine, the method of using the guards, devices and appliances required by these Regulations.

Duties of persons employed

14. — (1) Every person employed shall, while he is operating a woodworking machine—

(*a*) use and keep in proper adjustment the guards and devices provided in accordance with these Regulations and all such safeguards as are mentioned in Regulation 8;

and

(*b*) use the spikes, push-sticks, push-blocks, jigs, holders and back stops provided in accordance with these Regulations,

except (in cases other than those specified in the proviso to Regulation 7(1)) when, because of the nature of the work being done, the use of the said guards, devices or other safeguards is rendered impracticable.

(2) It shall be the duty of every person employed who discovers any defect in any woodworking machine or in any guard, device or appliance provided in accordance with these Regulations or in any such safeguard as is mentioned in Regulation 8 (being a defect which may affect the safe working of a woodworking machine) or who discovers that the floor or surface of the ground around any woodworking machine is not in good and level condition or is slippery, to report the matter without delay to the occupier, manager or other appropriate person.

Sale or hire of machinery

15. The provisions of section 17(2) of the principal Act (which prohibits the sale or letting on hire of certain machines which do not comply with the requirements of that section) shall extend to any woodworking machine which is for use in a factory and which is not provided with such guards or devices as are necessary, and is not so designed and constructed as, to enable any requirement of the following Regulations to be complied with, that is to say, Regulations 8, 16, 17(3) 21, 22, 24, 25, 26, 27, 28, 30, 31 and 39 in so far as the requirement applies to that woodworking machine.

THE CROSSCUT SAW

The main purpose of the Wadkin Bursgreen universal radial arm saw is to cross cut timbers to length (see figure 5.1). This is usually the first machine to be used when timber is brought into the machine shop, the operator cutting each piece to its required length before it moves on to the next machine. This machine can be obtained to take a saw with a maximum diameter of 250 or 300 mm. The former will be capable of cutting timber up to a thickness of 75 mm while the larger saw will cut up to a maximum of 100 mm. The maximum thickness will be reduced if the saw is tilted to make bevelled cuts.

The arm on which the saw unit is carried will swivel up to 45° in either direction allowing the saw to make angular cuts across the timbers. The saw unit travels along the arm to make a cut and is capable of being locked in any position along the arm. It can also be tilted up to an angle of 45° in either

direction and the arm on which it travels can be raised or lowered so that the depth of cut can be adjusted. The handle for raising or lowering the arm can be seen at the top of the pillar that carries the arm.

The 250 mm saw will cross cut timber up to approximately 380 mm wide and the 300 mm saw will cut material up to approximately 355 mm in width. Larger machines will cut timbers to larger dimensions.

Just below the handle which raises or lowers the arm can be seen a scale which allows the operator to swivel the arm to any required angle.

Another scale is fixed around the handle which the operator grips to make a cut. This allows the saw unit to be tilted to any required angle.

After checking that the isolator is in the 'off' position, the piece of timber to be cut is placed on the machine table with its edge resting against the fence and approximately in such a position that the saw is opposite to where the cut is to be made. The arm should then be raised or lowered according to the cut to be made. The isolator is then switched to the 'on' position and the 'on' button pressed to start the machine.

Holding the timber steady with the left hand, the handle in front of the saw unit should then be gripped with the right hand and the arm locking device released. The saw unit should then be drawn forward to allow the saw to make its cut having first adjusted the position of the timber so that the saw will cut to the line required. The saw unit is then pushed back to the rear of the arm and locked in this position. The 'stop' button should then be pressed to stop the machine and the isolator turned off. The timber can then be removed from the table.

As has already been indicated, the crosscut saw can perform a variety of work from square crosscutting to bevelled and splayed cuts. Some machines will allow the saw unit to be used for ripping, ploughing and moulding timber.

The letters in figure 5.1 indicate the following parts of the machine

a — Table; b — Pillar; c — Scale for swivelling arm; d — Arm; e — Saw carriage; f — Hand lever; g — scale for tilting saw; h — 'on/off' switch.

Figure 5.2 shows how the crosscut-saw bench is used for straight crosscutting — the saw cutting at right angles to the edges of the timber. The scale for obtaining the correct angle of cut is clearly seen in this illustration and also in figure 5.3, which shows the crosscutting saw set up for bevelled work.

A general view of the crosscutting machine set up for mitre cutting appears in figure 5.4 and figure 5.5 shows how the machine is used for compound angle cutting.

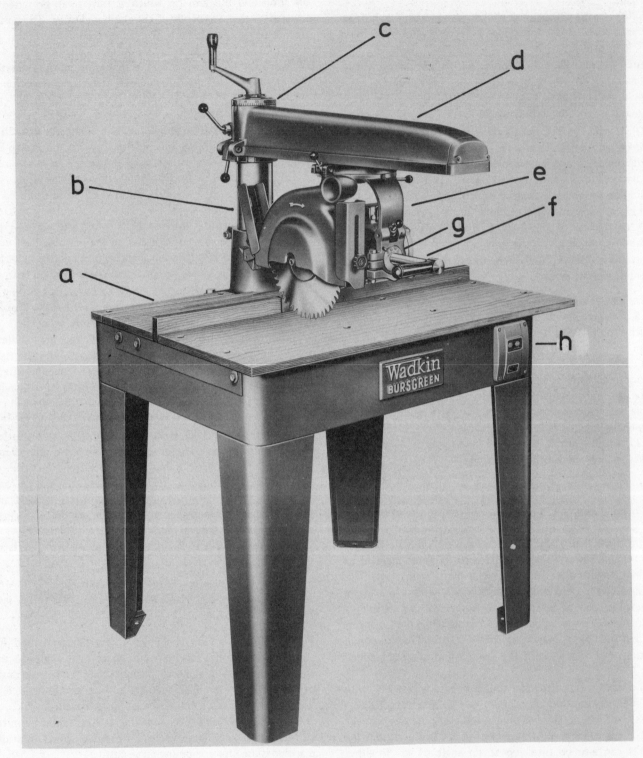

Figure 5.1

Figure 5.2

Figure 5.4

Figure 5.3

Figure 5.5

CIRCULAR-SAW BENCHES

After timber has been cut to the required length with a crosscut saw, the pieces are transferred to the circular saw bench for cutting roughly to width and thickness. The primary function of this machine is to *rip* timber; this means, to cut timber in the direction of its grain. To rip timber through its smallest dimension is called *flatting* and cutting through its widest dimension in the direction of the grain is called *deeping*.

THE WOODWORKING MACHINES REGULATIONS, 1971

Part III circular sawing machines

Guarding of circular sawing machines

16. — (1) That part of the saw blade of every circular sawing machine which is below the machine table shall be guarded to the greatest extent that is practicable.

(2) There shall be provided for every circular sawing machine a riving knife which shall be securely fixed by means of a suitable device situated below the machine table, be behind and in a direct line with the saw blade, have a smooth surface, be strong, rigid and easily adjustable and fulfil the following conditions:—

(*a* the edge of the knife nearer the saw blade shall form an arc of a circle having a radius not exceeding the radius of the largest saw blade with which the saw bench is designed to be used;

(*b*) the knife shall be capable of being so adjusted and shall be kept so adjusted that it is as close as practicable to the saw blade, having regard to the nature of the work being done, and so that at the level of the machine table the distance between the edge of the knife nearer to the saw blade and the teeth of the saw blade does not exceed 12 millimetres;

(*c*) for a saw blade of a diameter of less than 600 millimetres, the knife shall extend upwards from the machine table to a height above the machine table which is not more than 25 millimetres below the highest point of the saw blade, and for a saw blade of a diameter of 600 millimetres or over, the knife shall extend upwards from the machine table to a height of at least 225 millimetres above the machine table; and

(*d*) in the case of a parallel plate saw blade the knife shall be thicker than the plate of the saw blade.

(3) Without prejudice to the requirements of Regulation 18(2), that part of the saw blade of every circular sawing machine which is above the machine table shall be guarded with a strong and easily adjustable guard, which:

(*a*) shall be capable of being so adjusted and shall be kept so adjusted that it extends from the top of the riving knife to a point above the upper surface of the material being cut which is as close as practicable to that surface or, where squared stock is being fed to the saw blade by hand, to a point which is not more than 12 millimetres above the upper surface of the material being cut; and

(*b*) shall be capable of being moved horizontally and parallel to the saw blade and shall be kept so adjusted that the horizontal distance between the lowest point at the front of the guard and the teeth of the saw blade is not more than 12 millimetres:

Provided that in the case of circular sawing machines manufactured before the date of the coming into operation of these Regulations the requirements of sub-paragraph (*b*) of this paragraph shall not apply until five years after the said date.

(4) The guard referred to in the last foregoing paragraph shall have along the whole of its length a flange of adequate depth on each side of the saw blade and the said guard shall be kept so adjusted that the said flanges extend beyond the roots of the teeth of the saw blade. Where the guard is fitted with an adjustable front extension piece, that extension piece shall have along the whole of its length a flange of adequate depth on the side remote from the fence and the said extension piece shall be kept so adjusted that the flange extends beyond the roots of the teeth of the saw blade:

Provided that in the case of circular sawing machines manufactured before the date of the coming into operation of these Regulations the requirements of this paragraph shall not apply until five years after the said date and in the case of such machines, until the expiration of the said period, the said guard shall have along the whole of its length a flange of adequate depth on the side remote from the fence and shall be kept so adjusted that the said flange extends beyond the roots of the teeth of the saw blade.

Sizes of circular saw blades

17. — (1) In the case of a circular sawing machine the spindle of which is not capable of being operated at more than one working speed, no saw blade shall be used thereat for dividing material into separate parts which has a diameter of less than six-tenths of the diameter of the largest saw blade with which the saw bench is designed to be used.

(2) In the case of a circular sawing machine which has arrangements for the spindle to operate at more than one working speed, no saw blade shall be used thereat for dividing material into separate parts which has a diameter of less than six-tenths of the diameter of the largest saw blade which can properly be used at the fastest working speed of the spindle at that saw bench.

(3) There shall be securely affixed to every circular sawing machine a notice specifying the diameter of the smallest saw blade which may be used in the machine in compliance with paragraph (1) or (2) (as the case may be) of this Regulation.

Limitations on the use of circular sawing machines for certain purposes

18. — (1) No circular sawing machine shall be used for work which involves feeding a workpiece to the saw blade by hand and starting a cut otherwise than at the end of a surface of the workpiece.

(2) No circular sawing machine shall be used for cutting any rebate, tenon, mould or groove, unless that part of the saw blade or other cutter which is above the machine table is effectively guarded.

(3) No circular sawing machine shall be used for cross-cutting logs, branches or any material intended for firewood unless the material being cut is firmly held by a gripping device securely fixed to a travelling table.

Provision of push-sticks

19. — (1) A suitable push-stick shall be provided and kept available for use at every circular sawing machine which is fed by hand.

(2) Except where the distance between a circular saw blade and its fence is so great or the method of feeding material to the saw blade is such that the use of a push-stick can safely be dispensed with, the push-stick so provided shall be used:

(*a*) to exert feeding pressure on the material between the saw blade and the fence throughout any cut of 300 millimetres or less in length;

(*b*) to exert feeding pressure on the material between the saw blade and the fence during the last 300 millimetres of any cut of more than 300 millemetres in length; and

(*c*) to remove from between the saw blade and the fence pieces of material which have been cut.

Removal of material cut by circular sawing machines

20. — (1) Where any person (other than the operator) is employed at a circular sawing machine in removing material which has been cut, that person shall not for that purpose stand elsewhere than at the delivery end of the machine.

(2) Where any person (other than the operator) is employed at a circular sawing machine in removing material which has been cut, the machine table shall be constructed or shall be extended over its whole width (by the attachment of rollers or otherwise) so that the distance between the delivery end of the table or of any such extension thereof and the up-running part of the saw blade is not less than 1200 millimetres.

Part IV multiple rip sawing machines and straight line edging machines

Multiple rip sawing machines and straightline edging machines

21. — (1) Every multiple rip sawing machine and straight line edging machine shall be provided on the operator's side of the in-feed pressure rollers with a suitable device which shall be of such design and so constructed as to contain so far as practicable any material accidentally ejected by the machine and every such device shall extend for not less than the full width of the said pressure rollers.

(2) Every multiple rip sawing machine and straight line edging machine on which the saw spindle is mounted above the machine table shall, in addition to the device required to be provided under paragraph (1) of this Regulation, be fitted on the side remote from the fence with a suitable guard, which shall extend from the edge of the said device along a line parallel to the blade of the saw at least 300 millimetres towards the axis of the saw and shall be of such a design and so constructed as to contain as far as practicable any material accidentally ejected from the machine.

(3) In the case of multiple rip sawing machines and straight line edging machines manufactured before the date of the coming into operation of these Regulations, the requirements of this Regulation shall not apply until three years after the said date.

The machine shown in figure 5.6 is a Wadkin Bursgreen circular-saw bench. The parts of this machine are listed below

a Riving knife. This is horizontally adjustable to fit the size of saw. Its position at the back of the saw is to stop timber from binding while being cut and to guard the back edge of the saw blades.

b Top guard (vertically adjustable).

c Handle for adjusting the top guard.

d Front extension piece to the top guard. The top guard

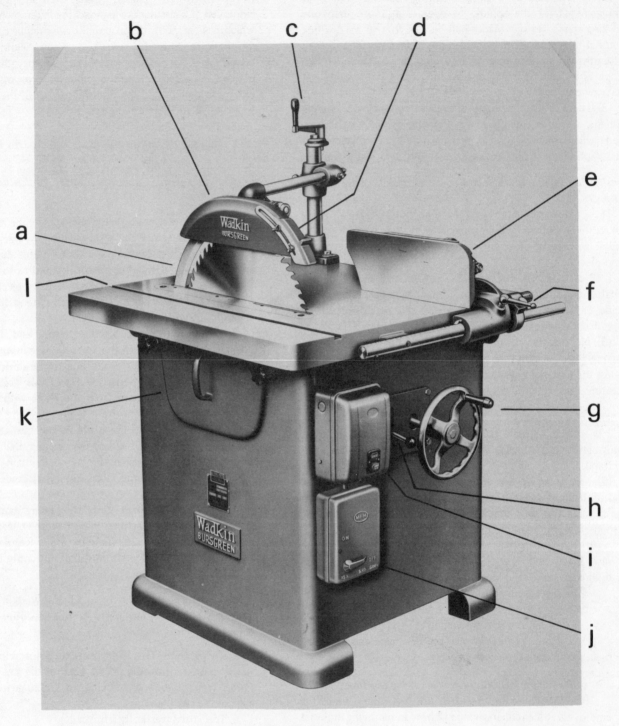

Figure 5.6

should be adjusted to allow the flanges on the sides of the guard to extend below the bottoms of the gullets of the teeth. It must also extend from the top of the riving knife. The front extension piece can be adjusted to cover the front edge of the blade when comparatively thin material is being cut.

e Fence. This may be canted over up to an angle of 45°

f Slide on which the fence is adjusted. The fence can be locked in any required position on the slide.

g Handle to adjust upward and downward saw action.

h Lever to lock the saw position after adjusting it for depth of cut.

i Push button control gear.

j Isolator switch.

k Cover of the opening in the machine casing to allow access to the saw spindle.

l Groove in the table in which a cross-cut fence can be located for cross-cutting timbers.

To rip a piece of timber on the circular-saw bench, the isolator switch must first be in the 'off' position. The top guard and fence must then be adjusted to the dimensions of the timber and, if necessary, the guard front extension must be raised or lowered to cover as much of the front edge of the blade as possible, but allowing the operator to see the front edge of the saw above the timber.

Next, the fence should be adjusted so that its distance from the inside edge of the saw blade is equal to the dimension required. The fence should then be locked in this position.

Remember that an allowance must be made on the finished dimensions of a piece of timber when it has been planed. Some machinists have their own ideas about the size of this allowance, but 5 mm allowed on both thickness and width when ripping should ensure the correct finished dimensions.

The isolator switch should then be turned to the 'on' position and the 'on' button pressed to start the machine.

The timber should be taken in both hands and moved up to the front edge of the saw, keeping its edge up against the fence. A small cut should be made and the timber withdrawn from the saw and the width of the cut checked. If satisfactory, the timber should again be placed on the table and cut, remembering to use the push stick (which should be close at hand to finish the cut. The timber should then be removed from the table, the 'off' button pressed and the isolator switch turned to the 'off' position.

DIMENSION-SAW BENCHES

Figure 5.7 shows a Wadkin tilting arbor dimension saw, capable of taking a 450 mm diameter saw and performing a large variety of cutting operations to very precise dimensions on timbers up to 140 mm in thickness. The guard gives full protection at every position of the saw and it is quickly and easily adjusted.

The riving knife is secured to the saw carriage which enables it to be located directly behind the saw each time the saw is tilted out of the vertical plane.

The various parts of this machine are

a — Sliding table; b — Mitre fence; c — Top guard assembly; d — Ripping fence; e — Handles for rise and fall and canting saw; f — Isolator switch; g — Foot-operated brake pedal.

This machine can be used for ripping and crosscutting timber and the saw carriage can be canted over up to an angle of 45° for bevelled and splayed cutting. When canted over to its maximum angle the saw will cut up to 100 mm in depth.

An additional advantage of a dimension saw is that the quality of the cut surfaces is almost equal to the quality of surfaces that are prepared on a planing machine. Hollow -ground saws are often used in the dimension-saw bench to produce the type of surface required.

A section of the table (from the saw blade to the side nearest to the operator) has a lockable sliding action the direction of which is parallel to the saw blade, thus making it possible to crosscut and to cut mitres and bevels with exceptional accuracy and ease of effort as compared with more orthodox types of machine.

The sliding table has several holes to enable the mitre fence to be secured in any position. The table is also slotted to receive a sliding or crosscutting fence when the use of the sliding table is unnecessary. This fence as well as the mitre fence have adjustable stops for accurate repetition work. It is also possible to draw the table away from the saw so that trenching heads can be fixed to the saw spindle. Ploughing and grooving can also be carried out on the machine by fixing the appropriate parts to the saw spindle.

Before making adjustments to any part of the machine the isolator switch should be turned to the 'off' position.

Figure 5.8 shows the use of the dimension-saw bench for crosscutting timber to length — note the stop on the arm attached to the crosscutting fence; it will also be seen that the sliding table is being used for this operation.

Figure 5.9 indicates how bevelled ripping is carried out on this machine.

Figure 5.10 illustrates the use of the mitre fence for making angled cuts with the aid of the sliding table.

Figure 5.11 shows the mitre fence (with the saw canted) for crosscutting compound angles.

Figure 5.12 illustrates mitre cutting with the crosscutting fence. (The sliding table is not used for this operation.)

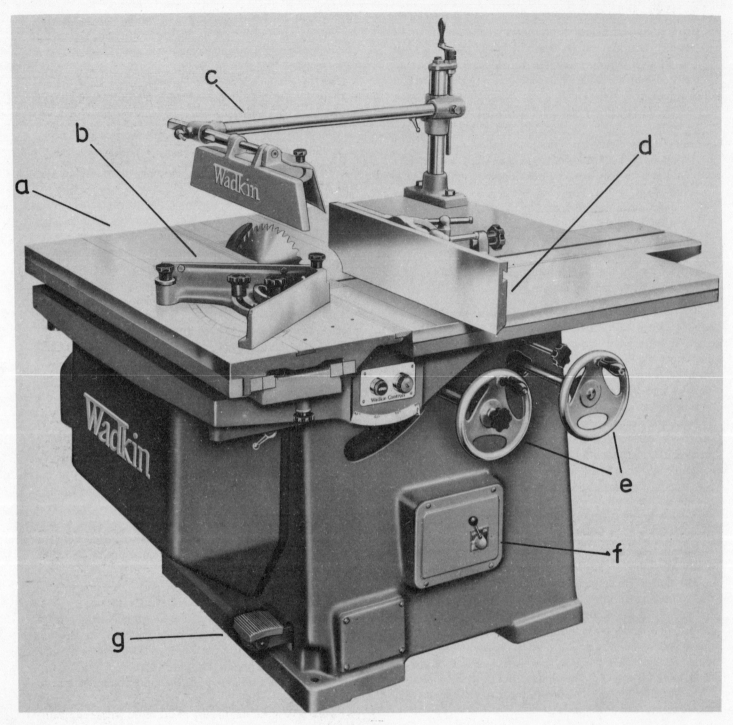

Figure 5.7

Figure 5.8

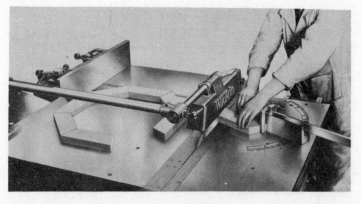

Figure 5.10

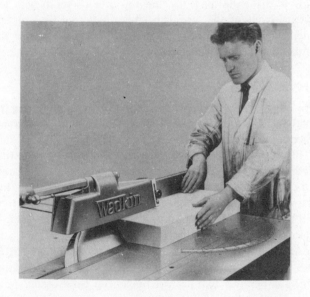

Figure 5.9

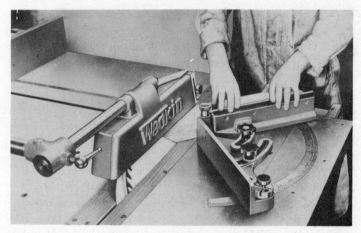

Figure 5.11

Figure 5.12

TILTING ARBOR-SAW BENCH

Another machine which can be classed as a dimension-saw bench is the tilting arbor-saw bench shown in figure 5.13. It takes a much smaller saw blade (maximum diameter 300 mm) but is still capable of performing an exceptionally large variety of work. It has a maximum depth of cut of 100 mm when cutting in the vertical position and when the saw has been tilted to its maximum of 45°, the depth of cut is reduced to 70 mm.

The top guard and riving knife form one unit and are secured to the saw carriage at the base of the riving knife; they rise, fall and cant with the saw. The table is grooved on both sides of the saw to take a crosscutting and mitring fence. Stops are supplied with the fence for repitition work. This machine, too, can be adapted for grooving, trenching and moulding.

The main parts of this machine are

a – Top guard and riving knife assembly; b – Ripping fence; c – Crosscutting fence; d – Rise and fall handle; e – 'On'/'Off' buttons; f – Saw canting handle.

Saw-blade fitting

Saw blades are mounted on to a spindle and between two collars; the rear collar is fixed to the spindle and the collar fixed to the front or outside of the saw is removable to allow the saw to be fitted and removed from the machine. The collars also support the saws. Some machines have a locating pin in the fixed collar which necessitates two holes being made in the saw blade. This pin assists the saw to take up the drive of the motor.

Circular-saw teeth

There are several types of saw teeth, the shapes of which are determined by the work to be done by the blade. Figure 5.14 shows the type of teeth used for rip sawing. These shapes of rip-saw teeth can vary considerably depending on the type of timber to be cut and on other factors that will be covered at a later stage. The various angles and names of the parts of the teeth are important and should, if possible, be memorized.

Pitch

Pitch is the distance between the points of two adjacent teeth. The terms, *face, point, top, heel* and *back* of each tooth have fairly obvious meanings.

The gullet, to remove the sawdust from the saw cut, is the space between each pair of teeth. Its depth is important and should be approximately half of the pitch and its area should be about the same area as each tooth.

Hook

The hook is the angle made by the face of a tooth and a line drawn from its point to the centre of the saw plate and, in the case of rip-saw teeth, this is a positive hook. The hook can be varied and more hook can be given to teeth for ripping softwoods, but there are limits because the cutting action of the saw is affected by the amount of hook.

Sharpness angle

This is the angle made by the top of a tooth and its face line. This angle can be reduced on saws used for cutting softwoods and made greater for hardwood ripping.

Clearance angle

This is the angle made by the top of each tooth with the cutting circle of the saw. This circle (indicated by a broken line) allows the top edge of each tooth to be clear of the timber during the cutting process.

Top bevel

This is the angle made on the top of each tooth during the sharpening of the saw plate. The top bevel is made in alternate directions on adjacent teeth (see figure 5.14).

Figure 5.15 shows the difference between crosscutting teeth and ripping teeth. In this case the hook has a negative angle and the clearance angle is much greater. During the sharpening of crosscutting teeth, a bevel is made on the front and back edges of each tooth and as in the case of rip teeth, in alternate directions on adjacent teeth.

Another type of crosscutting teeth is shown in figure 5.16; they are very similar to rip-saw teeth, but have a negative hook, as opposed to a positive hook. Top bevels again are in opposite directions and a face bevel is also given to these teeth.

Figure 5.17 shows novelty-type saw teeth, which are found on hollow-ground saws used where a good surface is required without having to use a planing machine. No set is required for this type of saw blade. The teeth comprise four crosscutting types with a leading tooth which appears to be of the rip-saw variety. This is not so and a glance at the illustration shows that the point of the last mentioned tooth is just below the cutting circle of the others. Its job is to rake out the saw dust

Figure 5.13

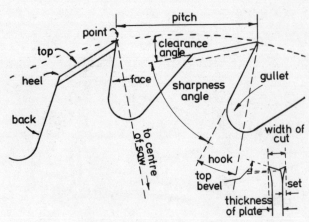

Figure 5.14   Ripsaw teeth

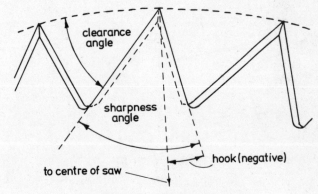

Figure 5.15   Crosscutting teeth

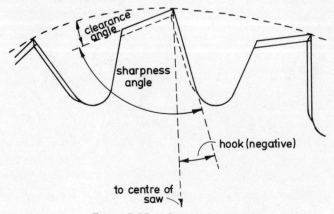

Figure 5.16   Crosscutting teeth

from the cut, hence its name — a raker tooth. Another saw tooth which is much used is the carbide-tipped tooth (figure 5.18). It is suitable for timbers which have a blunting effect on the teeth and for laminated plastics, as well as for general-purpose work which requires long periods of running without maintenance.

Figure 5.19 shows the various types of saw blades. a is a plate saw with a constant thickness. b is a hollow-ground saw which has a constant thickness at the centre and is ground off from the rim towards the centre on both sides. c shows a ground-off saw which has a fairly thick centre plate but is ground off near the rim to a very thin gauge on one side of the plate only. These saw blades are used for cutting thin boards up to a thickness of 6 mm. Because of its thinness the board is able to bend away from the saw as the cutting progresses. d shows a swage-saw plate which is tapered on one side (the fence side) only. It is used for cutting boards up to 19 mm in thickness. The saw shown in e — a taper-ground saw plate — is tapered on both sides of the blade and can be used for cutting a board down its thickness, producing two equally thick boards up to a maximum of 19 mm.

Sharpening teeth

When saw blades have been used over a period (the length of this period depends on the types of timber that have been cut) the teeth lose their efficiency and become blunt.

In this instance, we will deal only with teeth that are to be spring set; that is, where every other tooth is bent slightly to one side of the saw blade and the remainder are bent over in the opposite direction.

The first thing to do with a blunt saw (remembering that some of the teeth may have some flat edges where their points should be) is to bring every tooth on the blade down to the same cutting circle. To do this, with the blade in the saw, the machine should be switched on, with the top guard in position and correctly adjusted; then an emery stone is held lightly against the points of the teeth (figure 5.20) taking great care not to put much pressure on the saw. The stone is moved to the left and to the right to avoid grooves being cut in its surface. This operation will ensure that the points of the teeth will all be in the same cutting circle when the blade has been sharpened.

The next step, shown in figure 5.21, is to use a flat file to produce the top bevel on each tooth and, at the same time, to resharpen each point. After this has been done, a saw-setting tool (figure 5.22) is used for bending over the tops of each tooth to form the set which allows the blade to cut through a

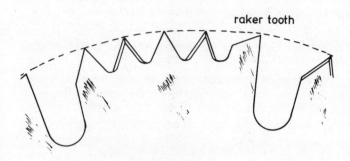

Figure 5.17   Novelty type teeth

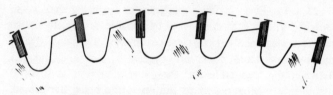

Figure 5.18   Carbide tipped teeth

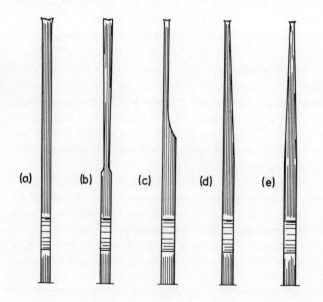

(a) (b) (c) (d) (e)

Figure 5.19   Types of saw

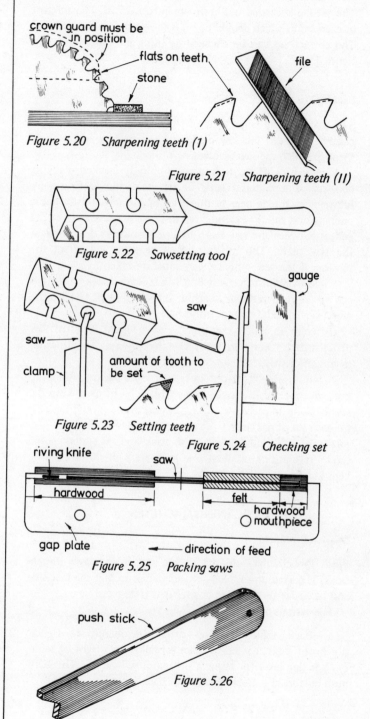

crown guard must be in position

flats on teeth

stone

Figure 5.20   Sharpening teeth (1)

file

Figure 5.21   Sharpening teeth (II)

Figure 5.22   Sawsetting tool

saw

clamp

saw

amount of tooth to be set

gauge

Figure 5.23   Setting teeth

Figure 5.24   Checking set

riving knife

saw

hardwood

felt

hardwood mouthpiece

gap plate

direction of feed

Figure 5.25   Packing saws

push stick

Figure 5.26

piece of timber and give a clearance on each side of the blade. The setting is carried out as shown in figure 5.23. The amount of each tooth which should be set is shown by the shaded area. The correct set can be checked by using the gauge shown in figure 5.24.

Packing for saws

Saw plates in the larger type of circular-sawing machines need *packing* between the saw blade and the opening in the table through which the saw revolves.

Figure 5.25 shows how saws should be packed. Packing consists of a material such as felt that should fit snugly between each side near to the front of the saw and the table opening and should extend from just below the bottom of the gullets between the saw teeth to a point near to the centre of the saw plate. Too much packing pressure will affect the tension of the saw — hence, care must be taken to avoid this.

Some machinists suggest that if felt is used as a packing it can be impregnated with machine oil which helps to keep the saw clean, cool and running smoothly.

Different thickness saw plates and different types of saw plate, such as taper saws, must have their own packing in order to run efficiently.

A mouthpiece is placed in front of the packing filling up the remainder of the space in the table. This helps to keep the saw packing in place. A different mouthpiece should be used for each set of packings.

Figure 5.26 illustrates a push stick and, as stated in the safety regulations, at least one push stick should always be kept at a saw bench.

PLANING MACHINES

Overhand planers

From the circular saw, the timber (cut to the sawn dimensions) is passed on to the overhand planer, so that the face-side and face-edge surfaces can be prepared (figure 5.27).

The various parts of this machine are

a — Back table; b — Top or bridge guard; c — Fence; d — Front table; e — Handwheel for adjusting height of table; f — Locking lever for table; g — Isolator switch; h — 'On'/'Off' push buttons; i — Locking lever for back table.

THE WOODWORKING MACHINES REGULATIONS 1971

Part VI planing machines

Limitation on the use of planing machines for cutting rebates etc.

23. No planing machine shall be used for cutting any rebate, recess, tenon, or mould unless the cutter is effectively guarded.

Cutter blocks for planing machines for surfacing

24. Every planing machine for surfacing shall be fitted with a cylindrical cutter block.

Table gap

25. — (1) Every planing machine for surfacing shall be so designed and constructed as to be capable of adjustment so that the clearance between the cutters and the front edge of the delivery table does not exceed 3 mm and the gap between the feed table and the delivery table is as small as practicable having regard to the operation being performed, and no planing machine which is not so adjusted shall be used for surfacing.

(2) In the case of planing machines manufactured before the date of the coming into operation of these Regulations, the requirements of the foregoing paragraph of this Regulation shall not apply until twelve months after the said date.

Provision of bridge guards

26. — (1) Every planing machine for surfacing shall be provided with a bridge guard which shall be strong and rigid, have a length not less than the full length of the cutter block and a width not less than the diameter of the cutter block and be so constructed as to be capable of easy adjustment both in a vertical and horizontal direction.

(2) Every bridge guard shall be mounted on the machine in a position which is approximately central over the axis of the cutter block and shall be so constructed as to prevent its being accidentally displaced from that position.

(3) In the case of planing machines manufactured before the date of the coming into operation of these Regulations, the requirements of this Regulation shall not apply until twelve months after the said date, and until the expiration of the said period such machines for surfacing shall be provided with a bridge guard capable of covering the full length and breadth of the cutting slot in the bench and so constructed as to be easily adjusted both in a vertical and horizontal direction.

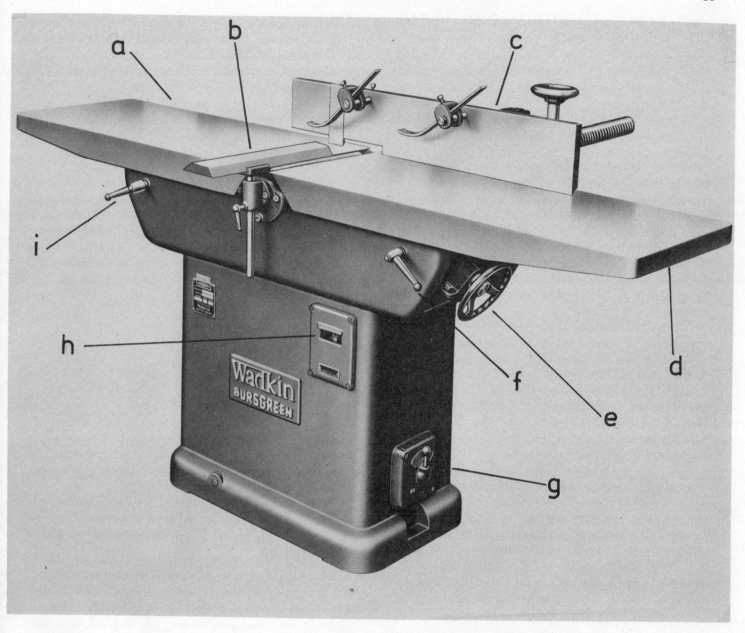

Figure 5.27

Adjustment of bridge guards

27. — (1) While a planing machine is being used for surfacing, the bridge guard provided in pursuance of Regulation 26 shall be so adjusted as to enable, so far as is thereby practicable, the work being done at the machine to be done without risk of injury to persons employed.

(2) Except as provided in paragraph (4) of this Regulation and in Regulation 29, when a wider surface of squared stock is being planed or smoothed, the bridge guard shall be adjusted so that the distance between the end of the guard and the fence does not exceed 10 mm and the underside of the guard is not more than 10 mm above the upper surface of the material.

(3) Except as provided in paragraph (4) of this Regulation, when a narrower surface of squared stock is being planed or smoothed, the bridge guard shall be adjusted so that the end of the guard is at a point not more than 10 mm from the surface of the said material which is remote from the fence and the underside of the guard is not more than 10 mm above the surface of the feed table.

(4) When the planing or smoothing both of a wider and of a narrower surface of squared stock is being carried out, one operation immediately following the other, the bridge guard shall be adjusted so that when a wider surface is being planed or smoothed the underside of the guard is not more than 10 mm above the upper surface of the material and, when a narrower surface is being planed or smoothed, the end of the guard is at a point not more than 10 mm from the surface of the said material which is remote from the fence.

(5) Except as provided in paragraph (6) of this Regulation, when the planing of squared stock of square cross section is being carried out, the bridge guard shall be adjusted in a manner which complies with the requirements either of paragraph (2) or of paragraph (3) of this Regulation.

(6) When the planing of two adjoining surfaces of squared stock of square cross section is being carried out, one operation immediately following the other, the bridge guard shall be adjusted so that neither the height of the underside of the guard above the feed table nor the distance between the end of the guard and the fence exceeds the width of the material by more than 10 mm.

(7) When the smoothing of squared stock of square cross section is being carried out, the bridge guard shall be adjusted in a manner which complies with the requirements either of paragraph (2) or of paragraph (3) or of paragraph (6) of this Regulation.

Cutter block guards

28. — (1) In addition to being provided with a bridge guard as required by Regulation 26, every planing machine for surfacing shall be provided with a strong, effective and easily adjustable guard for that part of the cutter block which is on the side of the fence remote from the bridge guard.

(2) In the case of planing machines manufactured before the date of the coming into operation of these Regulations, the requirements of the foregoing paragraph of this Regulation shall not apply until twelve months after the said date.

Provision and use of push-blocks

29. When a wider surface of squared stock is being planed or smoothed and by reason of the shortness of the material the work cannot be done with the bridge guard adjusted as required by Regulation 27(2), a suitable push-block having suitable handholds which afford the operator a firm grip shall be provided and used.

Combined machines used for thicknessing

30. That part of the cutter block of a combined machine which is exposed in the table gap shall, when the said machine is used for thicknessing, be effectively guarded.

Protection against ejected material

31. — (1) Every planing machine used for thicknessing shall be provided on the operator's side of the feed roller with a suitable device, which shall be of such a design and so constructed as to restrain so far as practicable any workpiece accidentally ejected by the machine.

(2) In the case of machines manufactured before the date of coming into operation of these Regulations, the requirements of this Regulation shall not apply until three years after the said date.

The overhand planer is fitted with a cutter block which has two or more cutters and revolves at a speed of 5,000 r.p.m. It comprises a front and back table which may be raised and lowered. They are adjusted by means of a screw and handwheel and move on inclined slides — the amount of adjustment can be seen on a scale. They can then be locked when the correct table heights have been obtained.

For the preparation of timber, the surface of the back table, which is the one farthest from the operator, is level with the cutting circle of the cutters in the block. The front table is lowered to below the cutting circle to obtain the required cut.

To protect the operator from accidents, the space between the tables is covered by a horizontally and vertically adjustable bridge guard on the working side of the fence. Another guard, fixed to the back surface of the fence, covers the cutter block when the fence has been brought nearer to the front edges of the tables for reasons which will be explained below.

The fence (which cants over to a maximum angle of 45° for bevelled work) is adjustable over the full width of the tables by means of a rack-and-pinion device that can be locked in any position. Some fences have pressure springs, which apply pressure to the top surface of the timber when it is being planed. A graduated scale allows the fence to be set to any desired angle.

To prepare one side and one edge of a piece of timber on an overhand-planing machine the following steps should be taken

(1) Check that the isolator switch is in the 'off' position.

(2) Check that the fence is set at right angles to the tables.

(3) Adjust the bridge guard so that the piece of timber can just pass underneath when the wide surface is being planed and that it can also just pass between the guard and fence when its edge is being prepared.

(4) Check that both tables are in their correct positions.

(5) Turn the isolator switch to the 'on' position and press the starter button. Allow the machine to reach its maximum speed before starting to plane the material.

(6) Place the timber on to the front table with the left hand on the top surface near to its leading edge. Use the right hand to the rear of the timber to feed the material towards the cutters.

(7) As soon as it is practicable, transfer the left hand to the top surface of the timber as it passes over the back table and maintain this pressure until the preparation of the surface of the timber has been completed. The material must be kept flat on the back table to produce a flat, straight piece of timber. It may be necessary to repeat this operation more than once to produce a flat surface.

(8) Lift the timber from the back table, select the edge to be prepared and repeat the process by passing the edge over the cutters, keeping the prepared surface nearest to the fence and pressed tightly to it. Maintain the pressure over the back table to produce a straight edge on the material.

(9) Remove the timber from the machine, press the stop button and turn the isolator switch to the 'off' position.

(10) If a deep cut has been made, readjust the front table to its original position to just below the cutting circle.

Figure 5.28 shows the process of surfacing a piece of timber.

Figure 5.29 shows how the machinist uses a thicknessing machine for bringing the timber to the required thickness

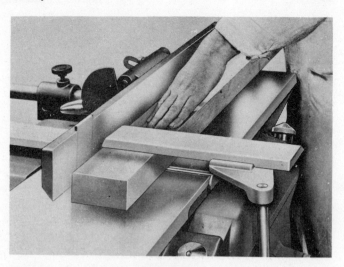

Figure 5.28

Figure 5.29

dimension. In this case the machine is of the combined variety, enabling surfacing and thicknessing to be done on the same machine.

Figure 5.30 shows how rebating is carried out on a thicknessing machine by lowering the front table to the depth of the required rebate. Note the guard over the cutterblock to the rear of the fence.

With the fence canted and the front table dropped to the required amount, bevelled work can be carried out on this machine (figure 5.31).

Tapering can also be carried out by dropping the front table and starting the cut by carefully lowering the leading end of the timber on to the back table (figure 5.32).

THICKNESSING MACHINE

When two sides of the timber have been prepared on the overhand machine, it is moved on to the thicknessing machine which will bring the material to its required thickness and width. Figure 5.33 shows a Wadkin thicknessing machine capable of planing material up to a maximum width of 310 mm and up to a thickness of 180 mm. Other, similar machines are capable of finishing timber to greater dimensions.

The cutter block has a diameter of 100 mm, revolves at a speed of 5,000 r.p.m. and is fitted with two or, if preferred, three cutters.

The various parts of this machine are

a — Rise and fall table; b — 'On'/'Off' buttons; c — Isolator switch; d — Thickness scale; e — Handwheel for adjusting table; f — Lock for table.

This machine is comparatively safe to use compared with the overhand planer or surfacer, since the cutter block is completely enclosed, however, it is still important to keep safety considerations in mind at all times.

The timber is fed into the machine after raising or lowering the table over which the timber passes (by turning the handwheel) to the required dimensions. The table can be locked in any position. The timber is pushed into the machine (prepared surface downwards) until taken up by the infeed rollers and automatically fed to the revolving cutters which reduce the thickness, so that the size of the material is equal to that indicated on the scale positioned at the end of the machine.

The feed speed on most machines can be regulated; on this machine, two speeds are obtainable — 4.5 m per minute and 9 m per minute. The slower speed will give a much better finish to the planed surface.

Figure 5.30

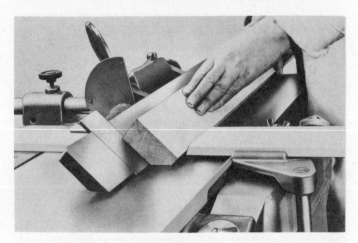

Figure 5.31

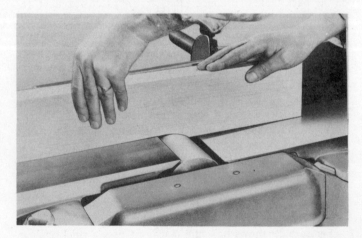

Figure 5.32

Figure 5.33

To avoid chattering during the thicknessing process, pressure bars are provided in front and behind the cutter block which apply pressure to the timber as it is passing below the revolving cutters.

As the timber approaches the rear end of the machine it is taken up by the outfeed rollers which allow it to come to rest clear of the cutters. The timber is then removed. To ensure that the timber will travel through the machine without becoming stationary, two antifriction rollers are provided which raise the material very slightly off of the table, thus reducing the friction as much as possible. The required timber dimensions are obtained on the thicknessing machine, in the following sequence.

(1) Ensure that the isolator switch is in the 'off' position.

(2) Select the required feed speed.

(3) Adjust the table to the required height to produce the finished dimension of the timber and lock in position. In order to reduce the timber to the required dimension it may be necessary to pass it through the machine several times. A rule should be used to find out the extent of the oversize.

(4) Switch on the isolator switch and press the 'on' button to start the machine.

(5) Place the leading end of the timber on to the table with the planed surface downwards and push forward carefully, allowing the infeed roller to take up the feeding of the timber towards the cutters.

(6) Remove the timber from the other end of the machine after it has been released.

(7) Press the 'stop' button to stop the machine and turn the isolator switch to the 'off' position.

COMBINED THICKNESSING AND SURFACING MACHINE

Figure 5.34 shows a planing machine on which all the timber-preparation processes can be carried out. A look at the illustration shows that this machine includes all the characteristics of the two previous machines.

The various parts of the machine are

a — Thicknessing table; b — Back surfacing table; c — Fence; d — Bridge guard; e — Front surfacing table; f — 'On'/'Off' buttons; g — Speed selector switch; h — Thicknessing scale; i — Isolator switch; j — Wheel and lock for thicknessing table.

Figure 5.35 shows the combination planer in use for surfacing.

Figure 5.36 shows the thicknessing table in greater detail and figure 5.37 shows the machine with the surfacing tables

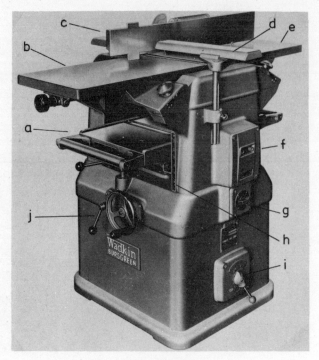

Figure 5.34

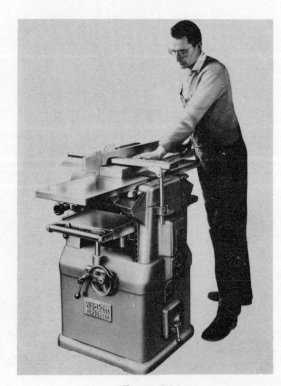

Figure 5.35

Figure 5.36

Figure 5.37

removed to reveal the serrated surface of the infeed roller to the thicknessing section of the machine; the cutter block and the outfeed roller, which can just be seen at the far end.

Figure 5.38a shows a section through a planing machine cutter-block and indicates the various angles set up by the cutter. Figure 5.38b shows an enlarged view of the cutting edge of a cutter used for the more difficult types of timber. The cutter has been given a front bevel — this has the effect of increasing angle b.

Figures 5.39 and 5.40 show two common types of cutter block, the first being a plate-type and the second being a wedge-type.

The setting of the irons in the block can be carried out in several ways. Figure 5.41 shows how this can be done by having a piece of timber on the back table — a mark indicating the edge of the table — and revolving the block so that the iron pushes the timber forward slightly. Another mark should be placed on the timber indicating the edge of the table. When adjusting the second cutter in the block, the same procedure should be followed and, if set on the same cutting circle as the first iron, it should push the timber forward exactly the same distance.

Figure 5.42 indicates another method using the Wadkin cutter setter.

Figure 5.43 shows the effect of feed speed — the speed at which the timber passes over the cutter. A slow speed (a) will give a much better finish than a fast speed (b), the waves produced by the cutters on the surface being smaller and shallower.

When the tables on an overhand machine are set correctly, the top surface of the back table should be in line with the cutting circle and the front table dropped to give the amount of cut required (figure 5.44).

Figure 5.45 shows that the back table has been set too high and figure 5.46 indicates that it has been set too low.

Figure 5.47 shows a piece of timber before it has been passed over a machine with the back table set too low. Indicate on the lower edge of the timber what would happen if this operation were carried out.

Figure 5.48 shows a section through a thicknesser planing machine. The anti-friction rollers set in the rise-and-fall table have their edges set just above the surface of the table. This reduces the friction of the timber on the table, allowing it to be fed through without difficulty. The infeed roller grips the timber and feeds it through below the cutters and the outfeed roller takes up the timber as it passes through. Pressure bars push down onto the timber and keep it steady throughout the cut.

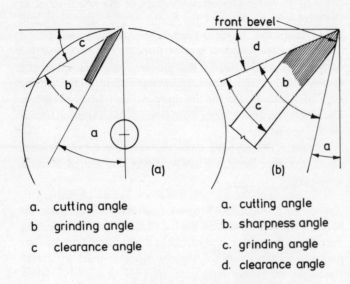

a. cutting angle
b grinding angle
c clearance angle

a. cutting angle
b. sharpness angle
c. grinding angle
d. clearance angle

Figure 5.38 · Planing cutters

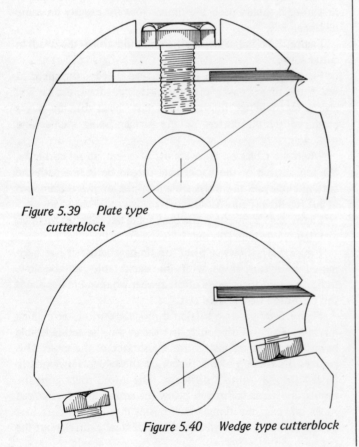

*Figure 5.39   Plate type
cutterblock*

Figure 5.40   Wedge type cutterblock

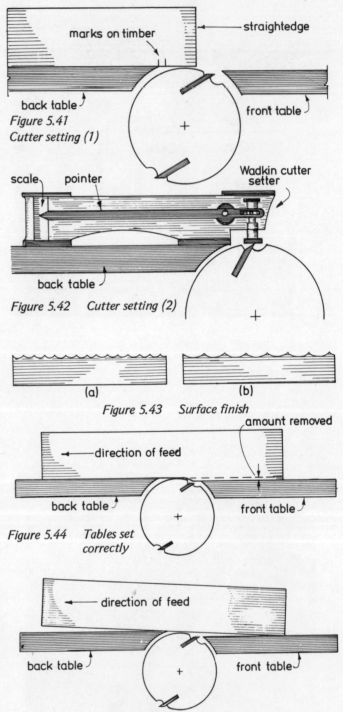

*Figure 5.41
Cutter setting (1)*

Figure 5.42   Cutter setting (2)

Figure 5.43   Surface finish

*Figure 5.44   Tables set
correctly*

Figure 5.45   Back table too high

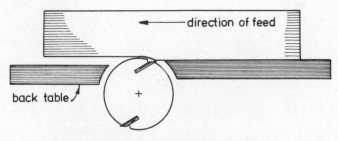

Figure 5.46   Back table lower than front

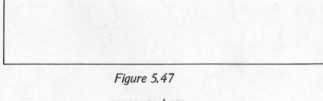

Figure 5.47

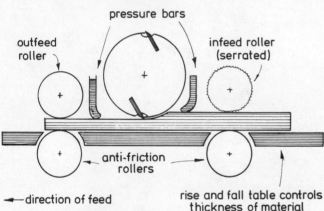

Figure 5.48   Section through thicknesser

MORTICING MACHINES

Two types of machine are in general use for the cutting of mortices, namely (i) the hollow chisel morticer and (ii) the chain morticer.

These machines can be obtained as individual machines or in combination, both types having their advantages and disadvantages. For instance, the chain morticer can produce mortices more quickly than a hollow chisel morticer; the mortices can be cut in one downward stroke, and much deeper mortices can be cut than by the chisel method. The disadvantages of the chain morticer are that if stub mortices are required, their lower ends will be rounded; also, very short mortices cannot be cut with a chain. Moreover, mortices cut

by a chain tend to split at the end from which the chain emerges from the timber.

The points in favour of the hollow chisel morticer are that it can cut stub mortices with square and flat lower ends and can produce clean and much shorter mortices than the chain morticer. Its disadvantages are: slowness of operation (several strokes having to be made as opposed to the single stroke of the chain morticer) and the cutting edges of the chisel and auger become blunt much sooner than the teeth on the chain morticer.

Hollow chisel morticer

A Wadkin hollow chisel morticer is shown in figure 5.49. The various parts of this machine are

a — Work table; b — 'On'/'Off' buttons; c — Adjustable stop bar; d — hand lever; e — Morticing head; f — Hollow chisel; g — Clamp to work table; h — Wheel for longitudinal movement of table; i — Wheel for lateral movement of table.

Figure 5.50 shows a front view of the Wadkin hollow chisel morticer.

Figure 5.51 shows the work-table controls. The large wheel is used for moving the table from left to right and the smaller wheel moves the table from back to front. This movement can be locked by the small lever seen near the wheel. Figure 5.52 shows the machine in use. Figure 5.53 is a close-up of the morticing head with chisel and auger located in the machine. Note the clearance between the lower ends of chisel and auger.

Figure 5.54 shows the work-table clamp. It has a downwards direction ensuring that the timber is clamped closely to the table and fence surfaces. Figure 5.55 shows a setting-out attachment for this machine for accurate repetition work without having to mark out each piece. The use of this attachment is shown in Figure 5.56.

To prepare a mortice on the hollow chisel morticer

(i) Check that the isolator switch is in the 'off' position.

(ii) Select the correct chisel and its auger and fit it into the machine, ensuring that the required amount of clearance between the bottom of the auger is obtained. This clearance should be approximately 2 mm. The chisel should be checked for squareness in the machine.

(iii) Clamp the timber on to the table with its face side to the fence.

(iv) Adjust the position of the table so that the chisel is in line with the mortice position.

(v) Cut the mortice starting from one end and working along to the other. Cut only about half way through the

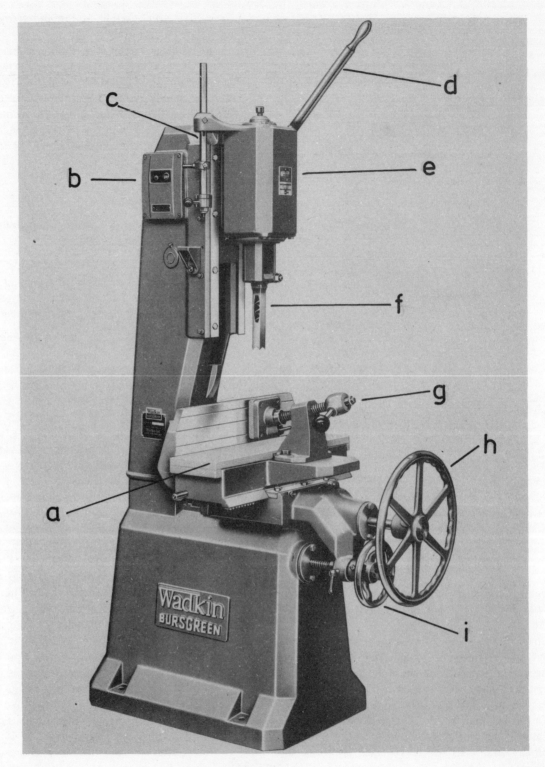

Figure 5.49

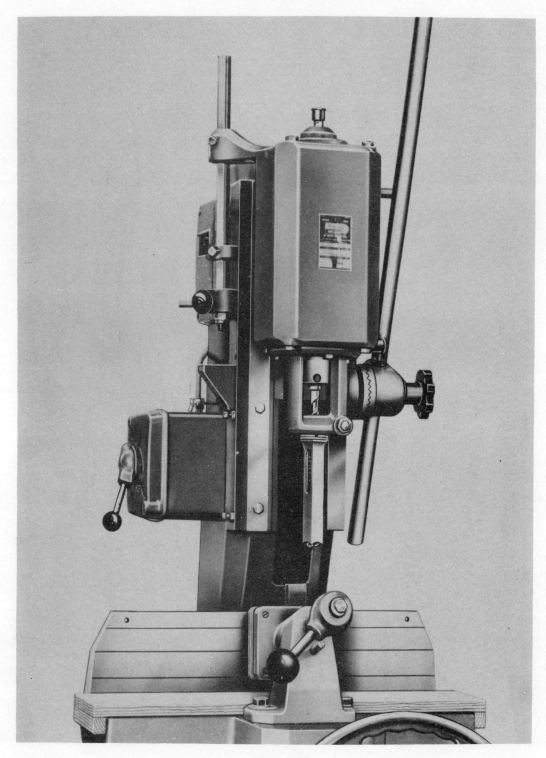

Figure 5.50

Figure 5.51

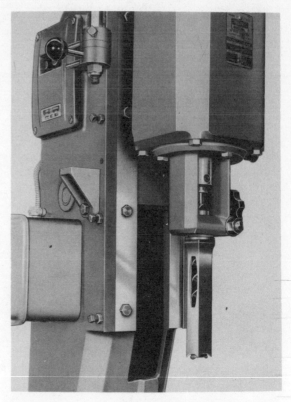

Figure 5.53

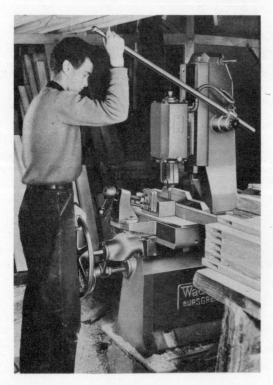

Figure 5.52

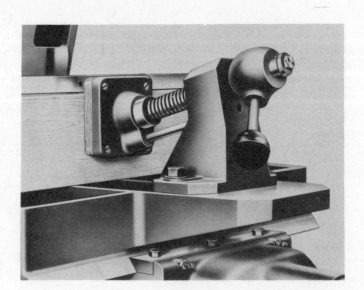

Figure 5.54

Figure 5.55

Figure 5.56

material. Turn the timber over and again clamp it on the table, still keeping the face side to the fence. Complete the cutting of the mortice. (Never attempt to move the position of the chisel while it is in the timber.)

(vi) Press the stop button and turn off the isolator switch. Remove the timber from the machine.

Figure 5.57 shows a hollow chisel that is square in section; passing through the chisel is an auger, shown in figure 5.58, which is similar in appearance to the twist bit the carpenter uses for drilling holes.

The chisel is sharpened to a cutting edge at the base of all of its four sides by means of the tool shown in figure 5.59. This tool is fixed in a hand brace with the chisel fixed in a vice. The turning action of the tool in the end of the chisel has a sharpening effect on the four cutting edges. A sharpening stone (figure 5.60) can also be used for sharpening hollow chisels.

The cutting angle of chisels is 35° when measured with their outer surfaces; this angle is reduced to 25° just beyond the cutting edge, as seen in figure 5.61. These bevels allow the timber to be cut easily by the chisel and also allow the auger to gather up the cut pieces, transfer them to the opening near the chisel top and eject them through this opening. Most of the cutting of the mortice is done by the auger, the chisel 'squares up' the round hole made by its drilling action.

When fixing the chisel and auger in the machine, it is necessary to allow a clearance of approximately 2 mm to their lower ends. If this clearance is not allowed, the resulting friction will cause tool overheating and loss of efficiency.

Both the chisel and the auger are fitted into the machine by means of collets (figures 5.62 and 5.63). The opening in the collet for the auger must line up with the flat near to the auger top. The collet for the chisel is of the split type which closes and grips the chisel when the two are placed in the machine.

The chisel and auger assembly, using the correct collets for each, are placed in the machine, the chisel being temporarily fixed first with its shoulders 2 mm, say, from its mounting. The auger should then be pushed up as far as possible into its place in the machine and tightened. The chisel is then loosened and pushed up tight into its mounting and fixed after making sure that its back surface is parallel to the fence of the machine. It will then be seen that the chisel and auger have the required clearance at the cutting edges.

When the machine is running, a small amount of oil should be injected regularly through the chip opening in the chisel to keep the chisel and auger working smoothly and efficiently.

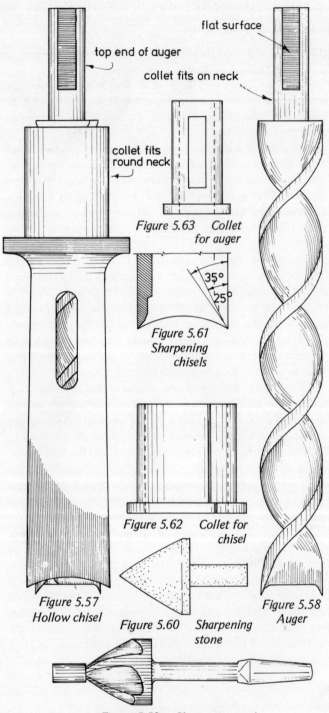

top end of auger

collet fits on neck

flat surface

collet fits round neck

Figure 5.63   Collet for auger

35°
25°

Figure 5.61 Sharpening chisels

Figure 5.62   Collet for chisel

Figure 5.57 Hollow chisel

Figure 5.60   Sharpening stone

Figure 5.58 Auger

Figure 5.59   Sharpening tool

The chain morticer

The chain consists of a series of links with teeth which have been sharpened to a cutting edge. The chain is driven by a sprocket in an anti-clockwise direction. It passes downwards and round a guide bar that can be adjusted for the correct chain tension. When the correct tension has been applied to a chain, it should be just possible to push a 6 mm dowel between the guide bar and the chain. The lower end of the guide bar (round which the chain travels) is fitted with a wheel to allow the chain to travel easily (figure 5.64).

The shape of the teeth is shown in figure 5.65 which includes a view of the teeth looking down on to their cutting edges. The pitch of the teeth is also shown — it is the distance between the cutting edges of two adjacent outer links or, as seen in the illustration, the distance between the two rivets below the cutting edges to two adjacent outer links.

There are three different pitches to mortice-machine chains, which are used, with their own sprockets, to cut mortices of various sizes: pitch 22.6 mm for large mortices; 15.7 mm for medium; 13.7 mm for smaller mortices. The teeth cut away the wood when the chain enters the timber. Fairly deep mortices can be cut with chains because of the depth of the guide bar. As the chain enters the wood, the chain guard comes down and rests on the top surface of the wood while the chain cuts to the required depth.

The chip breaker, which is situated at the point where the chain makes its exit from the timber, also rests on the top surface of the timber and prevents splitting of the fibres by the chain action. Even so, slight splitting of the fibres occurs at this point.

Figure 5.66 shows a mortice-chain assembly complete with sprocket and guide bar as well as the position of the chip breaker.

Most chain morticing machines have an attachment for sharpening the cutting edges to the links. It includes a device for mounting the chains to the attachment. Depending on the pitch of the chain, sprockets can be fixed to the device which includes a ratchet which brings each tooth into position so that it can be ground with a specially shaped grinding wheel. This wheel will ensure that the correct hook is maintained on each tooth. The hook should be approximately 25° (figure 5.67).

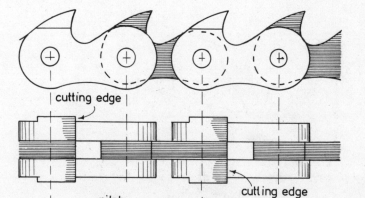

Figure 5.65   Details of mortice chains

cutting edge

cutting edge

pitch

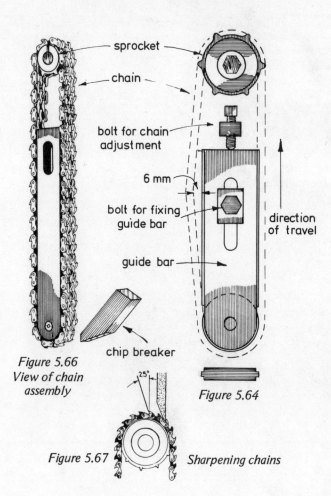

sprocket

chain

bolt for chain adjustment

6 mm

bolt for fixing guide bar

guide bar

direction of travel

chip breaker

Figure 5.66 View of chain assembly

Figure 5.64

25°

Figure 5.67   Sharpening chains

BANDSAWS

Narrow bandsawing machines

The Wadkin band saw (figure 5.68) has 610 mm diameter top and bottom pulleys and can take saws up to a maximum of 30 mm in width. The top saw-guides can be raised to a maximum of 330 mm; hence work can be cut up to this depth. The distance from the saw to the body of the machine is 560 mm thus material up to this width can be accommodated between the saw and body. The table (760 mm square) can be canted up to an angle of 45° and the saws travel at a speed of 1370 m per minute. These details relate to this particular machine, but they should give the reader a good idea of the work a bandsawing machine is capable of performing, allowing for variations in machine size.

THE WOODWORKING MACHINES REGULATIONS, 1971

Narrow band sawing machines

Narrow band sawing machines

22. – (1) The saw wheels of every narrow band sawing machine and the whole of the blade of every such machine, except that part of the blade which runs downwards between the top wheel and the machine table, shall be enclosed by a guard or guards of substantial construction.

(2) That part of the blade of every such machine as aforesaid which is above the friction disc or rollers and below the top wheel shall be guarded by a frontal plate which is as close as is practicable to the saw blade and has at least one flange at right angles to the plate and extending behind the saw blade.

The various parts of this machine are

a – Top pulley guard; b – Tracking device; c – Saw-tensioning wheel; d – Saw blade front guard; e – Top saw-guides assembly; f – Fence; g – Worktable; h – Bottom pulley guard.

The bandsaw is used mainly for curved work, although straight cutting is also carried out on this machine. Most machines are supplied with a straight fence that can be fitted on either side of the saw. Saws of different widths are used for the assorted jobs that are carried out on the bandsaw – the widest saws are used for straight work and for curved work of large diameter; the saw width decreases as the diameter of work decreases; as a rule, the widest saw capable of doing the required work should be used.

Jigs should also be used where necessary. It is particularly dangerous to cut round items on a bandsaw unless they are

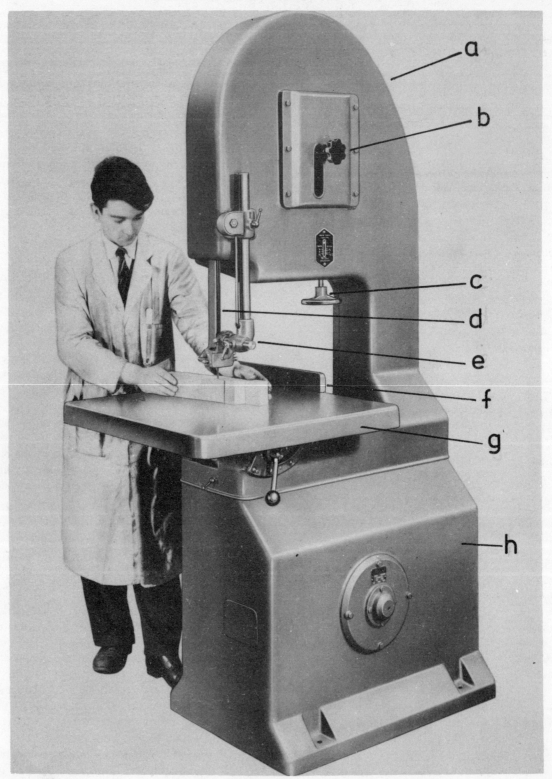

Figure 5.68

securely held in a device which will prevent them from turning with the action of the saw.

To operate the bandsaw the following steps should be followed

(i) Ensure that the isolator switch is in the 'off' position.

(ii) Check that the saw does not require changing because of bluntness and that its width is correct for the work required.

(iii) Check that the correct saw tension has been applied and, if necessary, adjust the tension, by means of the adjusting wheel located below the top pulley.

(iv) Check that the saw guards are adjusted correctly. If necessary, adjust the saw guards so that they are immediately behind the saw gullets and just clear of the saw sides.

(v) Adjust the guard in front of the saw blade facing the operator so that only that part of the saw which is to perform the work is protruding below the guard.

(vi) Turn the isolator switch to the 'on' position and start the machine by pressing the 'on' button.

(vii) Check that the saw is running in the centre of the rim of the top pulley and if an adjustment is needed, check the saw tension afterwards.

(viii) Make the cut, keeping the hands well clear of the saw blade and after completing the cut stop the machine and turn the isolator switch to 'off' position.

Narrow bandsawing machines

A simple description of a bandsaw and of its action is that it has a thin, narrow strip of steel, with saw teeth formed on its front edge, which travels around two revolving wheels or pulleys and passes through a horizontal table onto which the work is placed for cutting. Its main use is to cut curved shapes, but it can perform other work too.

Figure 5.69 is a line diagram of a narrow bandsaw. The saw is seen to pass round the top and bottom pulleys and in its downward movement passes through a table which can be set, on most machines, at any angle up to 45°. This enables splayed or bevelled work to be done. The rims of the pulleys have rubber tyres over which the saw blade passes. The top pulley can be raised or lowered by an adjusting wheel to allow the correct tension to be applied to the saw and also to assist in its removal. Another device attached to the top pulley ensures that the blade runs across the centres of the pulley rims.

Guides are positioned above and below the work table; their function is to support the sides of the saw blade during the cutting operation. Positioned at the rear of the blade and near to the top guides is a thrust wheel which supports the back of the saw when it is in operation.

Figure 5.70 shows the shape of the teeth on a small section of a narrow-bandsaw blade. Narrow-bandsaw blades can be obtained in widths from 6 to 38 mm, there are more teeth in a 6 mm blade than there are in a blade of greater width. For instance, there can be as many as 28–30 teeth per 100 mm run of the blade on the narrowest of blades and approximately 14 teeth per 100 mm run on the widest type.

The teeth are sharpened with a three-cornered file; each tooth is sharpened with the direction of the file stroke at right angles to the blade. The setting is then done as in the case of hand saws — every other tooth is set in one direction and the others set over to the other side of the blade. Figure 5.71 also shows the amount of set.

A wooden mouth piece is provided where the saw blade passes through the table. A vertical section through the table and mouthpiece is shown in figure 5.72a. Figure 5.72b shows the mouthpiece which fits flush with the top surface of the table.

Figure 5.73a shows an elevation of the saw guides and thrust wheel and a side view of the same components appears in figure 5.73b.

The guides should be positioned so that they are just clear of the saw blade. The fronts of the guides should be located just behind the gullets of the teeth. When using the bandsaw, the top guides should be lowered or raised, as the case may be, so that they are as close to the work as practicable.

The thrust wheel (positioned behind the saw blade) supports the blade during a cut and should come into contact with the blade only during the cutting operation. When the pressure is taken off the blade will run forward slightly to clear the thrust wheel.

Care must be taken when cutting shapes on the bandsaw. Small curves require a narrow saw blade. For instance, to cut a circular disc of diameter 400 mm requires a sawblade width not greater than 25 mm and a disc of diameter 75 mm requires a blade that is not wider than 9 mm.

LATHES

Wood-turning lathe

A Wadkin wood-turning lathe capable of producing a large variety of items to a high quality finish is illustrated in figure 5.74.

The main parts of this machine are indicated below

a — Headstock with inside and outside faceplates; b — Tail-

Figure 5.70   Bandsaw teeth

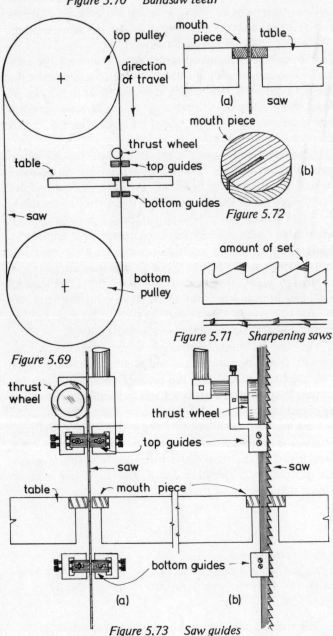

Figure 5.69

Figure 5.72

Figure 5.71   Sharpening saws

Figure 5.73   Saw guides

stock; c — Bed; d — Motor; e — Pedal for releasing and re-applying tension to driving belt; f — Tool shelf; g — Tool rest; h — Push button control.

The machine has four pulley speeds of 425, 800, 1400 and 2300 r.p.m. The pulleys are exposed by opening the access cover above the headstock. The headstock has a V-belt drive and the motor is automatically cut out when the access cover is raised or when the brake is applied. When the speed of the spindle is to be changed, the foot pedal near the floor is depressed, thus releasing the tension, the belt is transferred to the appropriate pulleys and the pressure on the pedal released to re-apply the tension.

The maximum distance between the centres of the head and tail stocks is 915 mm, but this figure varies considerably for other makes of machine.

The tail stock is able to slide to any position on the machine bed and can be locked securely to suit the material to be turned. The tool rest can also be positioned and locked where required along the length of the bed.

The spindle is screwed at both ends to take faceplates and is bored out at the inner end for driving centres. Below the spindle and at its outer end is another tool rest which is used, with the faceplate at that end, for turning fairly large circular work. On large machines the tool rest at the outside end of the pulley is supported on a heavy metal rest which stands on the floor beside the machine.

Accessories

Sets of turning chisels can be obtained for producing the many shapes obtainable on a wood lathe. They can be classed as turning gouges, (curved section) or turning chisels (flat section). Some turning chisels are illustrated in figure 5.75.

Gouges (figure 5.75) which are used mainly for removing the surplus wood from the work or forming concave surfaces are ground on their outside edges similarly to an outside-ground joiner's gouge, which is often called a scribing gouge, and can be obtained in various sizes.

Chisels come in a variety of shapes — round, square, bevelled, double bevelled and, in fact, many turners shape their own chisels to suit their particular requirements (figure 5.75a—d). Another cutting tool, which can be classed as a chisel is the parting-off tool (figure 5.75).

Figures 5.76 to 5.83 show the various items required for holding the material between the head and tail stocks.

Figure 5.76 is a face plate that is obtainable in various sizes and is used to suit the size of the job. Several holes are drilled in the plate so that the work can be fixed to it. The centre hole

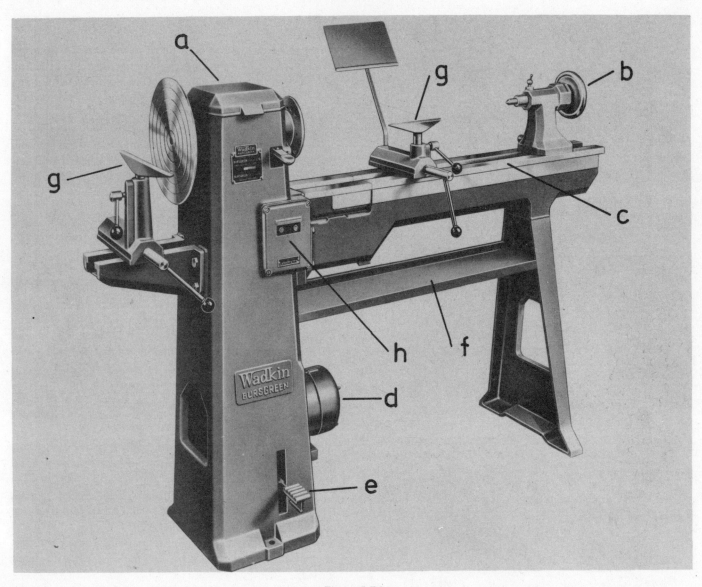

Figure 5.74

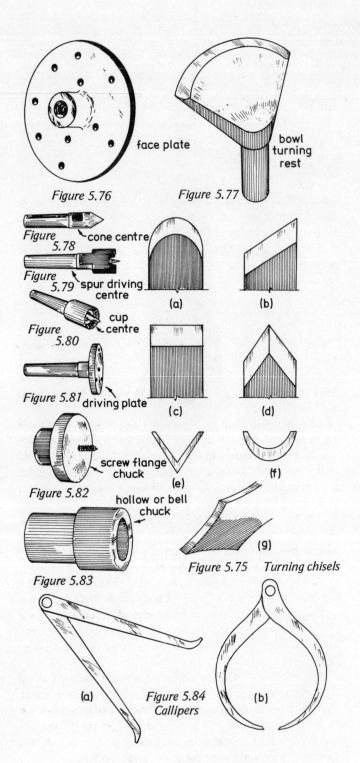

Figure 5.76

Figure 5.77

Figure 5.78 cone centre

Figure 5.79 spur driving centre

(a)

(b)

Figure 5.80 cup centre

Figure 5.81 driving plate

(c)

(d)

screw flange chuck

(e)

(f)

Figure 5.82

hollow or bell chuck

Figure 5.83

Figure 5.75   Turning chisels

(g)

(a)

Figure 5.84 Callipers

(b)

in the plate is threaded so that it can be screwed on to the end of the spindle.

The work must be securely fixed to the face plate to avoid accidents during turning and the material must be concentric with the plate. The face plate is used for instance when turning wooden bowls. The bowl-turning rest (figure 5.77) is used for shaping the concave inner surface of a bowl.

The cone centre (figure 5.78) is usually supplied in a pair, one being used in the headstock and the other at the opposite end of the work, in the tailstock. They hold the work at each end but do not revolve with it; hence it is occasionally advisable to run some thin machine-oil between each centre and the work to avoid friction.

The four-spur driving centre (figure 5.79) is used in the head stock. Its prongs are forced into the work with the centre point in the centre of the work. In this instance, the centre revolves; thus there is no friction between it and the work.

The cup centre (figure 5.80) is similar to the spur-driving centre, but is round in shape with a centre point for locating the centre of the work.

The screw-point driving plate shown in figure 5.81 is used when it is necessary to turn small items that cannot be held between conical centres. A hole in the centre of the plate is drilled to take a wood screw that is driven into the work through the shank of the plate so that the centre of the work can be located. Additional holes are provided in the plate for securing the work.

The screw-flange chuck (figure 5.82) is screwed on to the headstock spindle and is used for turning small pieces of work, held by the taper screw.

The hollow or bell chuck, shown in figure 5.83, is screwed on to the spindle of the head stock and is bored with a tapered hole which holds the work. The end of the work to be turned is first shaped to a similar taper to that of the chuck and then driven into the chuck which will grip the work while it is being turned.

Marking and checking dimensions of turned pieces are important steps during the production of work on a lathe. Dimensions can be marked on a revolving piece of round wood by means of a pair of dividers. These can be opened to the dimension to be marked on the timber and by resting the dividers on the tool rest, marks can be made with the sharpened points of the dividers.

The inside and outside callipers (figure 5.84) are used for checking inside and outside dimensions.

6. IRONMONGERY

The selection of ironmongery by the individual woodworker is necessary from time to time and a knowledge of the various items available is essential if the correct choice is to be made.

HINGES

Figures 6.1–6.5 illustrate only a few of the many types of hinges available, but they do represent those in common use.

The strap hinge shown in figure 6.1a is used for heavy types of gates, garage doors, and similar jobs. It is fixed by screwing it on to the face of the gate or doorway with the addition of one bolt which should have a round head to prevent the hinge being removed from the front. The bolt fits in the square hole near to the pivot end of the hinge and should have square shoulders below the head to prevent it from being turned. The pivot or pin can be obtained in two forms — for building into brickwork (figure 6.1b) or to be screwed to adjacent woodwork (figure 6.1c).

The hinge which is probably used more often than any other, is called *butt hinge* (figure 6.2a). It is used for doors, windows, cupboards, cabinets, boxes, etc. It consists of two leaves connected by a knuckle. Each leaf is let into one half of the two members to be hinged together and the marking out of the recess to receive a leaf is shown in figure 6.2b.

The dimensions marked x and y on the drawing are important if binding of the hinge is to be prevented.

Figure 6.3 illustrates the type of hinge that would be used if the door had to open over a fitted carpet or an uneven floor. This is a *rising butt hinge* and is fitted in a similar way to the common butt hinge, but in this case a small portion must be removed from the top of the door farthest from the hinge side to prevent the door binding on the frame when it rises as it opens.

Figure 6.4 shows a *casement hinge* which is comparatively new to the industry. It is used for hinging casement windows to their frames when it is necessary to clean the outer surfaces of the glass panels. The casement, when open, will be well clear of the frame at the hinge side, allowing an arm to be passed through the gap. This hinge is similar to the Parliament hinge shown in chapter 12.

The *backflap*, (figure 6.5) is a cheap type of hinge used for such work as hinging the two halves of a step ladder. The two leaves are screwed to the surfaces of the timber.

LOCKS

Locks for doors are used for security purposes, but most locks have two functions, first to give security — which means it must be impossible for anyone to gain entry unless he has the key — second to keep the door closed without having to use the key to lock it.

The cheapest form of lock — the *rim lock* — is shown in figure 6.6. It is fixed to the face of the door by screws through the four holes shown in the illustration. In addition to the bolt, which is thrown over by means of a key, the lock also has a latch which enables the door to be kept closed without using the key.

The *box staple* (figure 6.7) is screwed to the door frame — its function is to receive the bolt and latch. This is not a lock to be recommended, because it is unsightly and can easily be removed from the door by the means of a screwdriver.

The *mortice lock* (figure 6.8) is used most extensively for internal and external doors. The body of the lock fits into a mortice which has to be cut in the edge of the door, as shown in figure 6.9b. The plate on the edge of the body of the lock fits into a recess so that it is flush with the surface of the edge of the door.

The marking out of the mortice and recess is shown in figure 6.9a, the mortice being cut first by using a twist bit to drill out most of the timber and finishing it with a chisel and mallet. The positions of the keyhole and spindle for the key and handle must be carefully marked on one surface of the door and checked before attempting to cut the holes.

The *striking plate*, (figure 6.8) is recessed into the face of

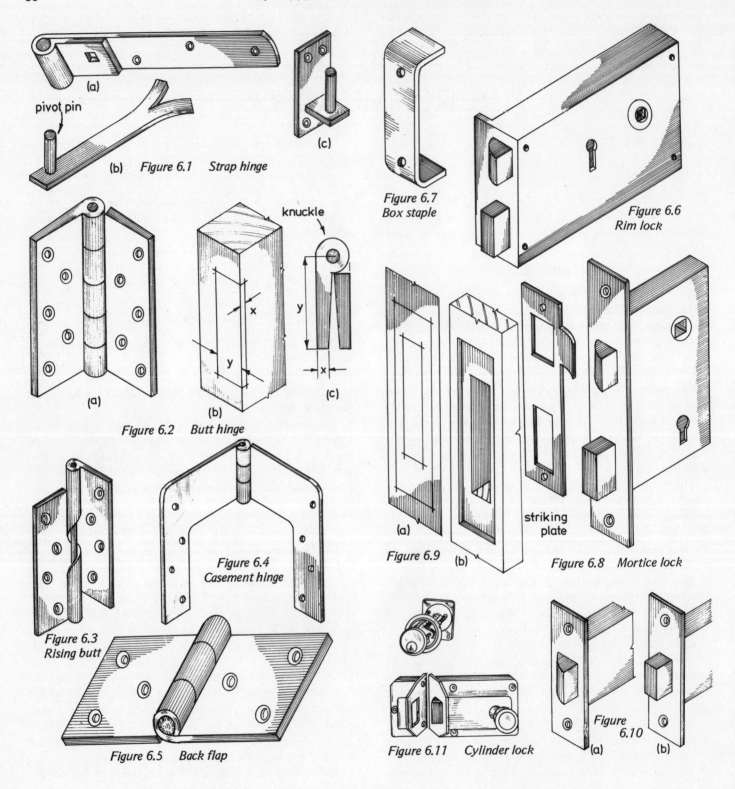

pivot pin

(a)

(b)   *Figure 6.1   Strap hinge*

(c)

Figure 6.7
Box staple

Figure 6.6
Rim lock

knuckle

x

y

y

x

(a)   (b)   (c)

Figure 6.2   Butt hinge

striking
plate

(a)   (b)   *Figure 6.8   Mortice lock*

Figure 6.9

Figure 6.4
Casement hinge

Figure 6.3
Rising butt

Figure 6.5   Back flap

Figure 6.11   Cylinder lock

Figure
6.10
(a)   (b)

the rebate in the door frame and receives the bolt and latch. The timber of the frame has to be cut away behind the openings in the striking plate to allow adequate depth for the latch and bolt.

Figure 6.10a and b shows two other forms of mortice lock. Figure 6.10a is a *mortice latch* for doors which are not required to be locked for security reasons and figure 6.10b shows a *mortice dead lock* that is fitted to doors that are usually kept locked at all times.

Figure 6.11 shows the type of lock found on most external doors. It is the *cylinder* lock which, like the rim lock, is screwed to the inside surface of the door. The front of the cylinder portion, seen at the top of the illustration, fits on the outside face of the door, the remainder passing through a hole that has to be drilled in the door, and engages the body of the lock on the rear surface. The lock is really a latch which requires a key to gain access from outside. The illustration also shows the box staple that is screwed to the door frame.

NAILS

There are many kinds of nail available and careful consideration must be given to the choice of a nail for a particular job.

Figure 6.12a—j shows the nails which are commonly used at present.

The *French wire nail* (a) is more of a carpenter's nail than a joiner's nail. It is round in section and has only reasonable gripping qualities. It is used for rough work such as formwork, packing cases, roof work, nailing floors joists to plates, etc.

The *oval brad* (b) is more of a joiner's nail because if it is used properly its shape tends to prevent timber from splitting. It is oval in section, with a head of similar shape, which allows it to be punched below the surface of the timber without doing too much damage.

A *floor brad* (c) is used for nailing floorboards to joists. It is wedge shaped, which gives it good gripping qualities. Its leading edge is blunt which tears away the fibres of the boards when it is driven through and so helps to prevent splitting.

The *lost-head nail* (d) is also used for flooring but is usually employed for fixing secretly nailed boards, the nail giving fairly good security. It can be driven home with the head finishing below the timber surface without too much damage to the fibres at the surface. It is also used for joinery purposes for the same reasons.

The *panel pin* (e) is a joiner's nail, used on fine work where strength is not important, such as fixing mouldings around panels.

The *roofing nail* (f) is used mainly for fixing corrugated sheets to roof timbers. Its spiral thread is similar to that of a metal screw.

The *wall nail* (g) is used for fixing metal items to walls, being driven home through a brickwork joint.

The *serrated nail* (h) is a fairly new type; it is used where high gripping properties are required, such as in timber structural work.

The *clout nail* (i) is employed, for instance, for fixing bituminous felt to flat roof surfaces, since its large flat head prevents tearing of the material at the nailing point.

The *fibre-board nail* (j) is used for fixing hardboard and other thin fibre-board sheets to framing. It is made from a non-ferrous metal and it is possible to strike the head of the nail to below the sheet surface without having to use a nail punch.

k, l and m show how the shapes of nails affect their gripping or holding powers. Figure 6.12k shows what happens when a round wire nail is used. Only slight deviation of the fibres occurs whereas in l the fibres around a serrated nail tend to get behind the serrations to resist the nail's withdrawal. The floor brad (m), although not altering the fibres to a large extent, has good gripping powers because of its wedging action.

Use of nails

The type of nails to be used and the timber through which they are to be driven, must both be considered before the work is commenced.

For instance, figure 6.13 shows what may happen to a piece of solid timber when a wire nail is driven through it. It will probably split, especially if the nailing is near to one of its ends. The correct way to deal with this problem is to drill a pilot hole first.

Oval brads can usually be used safely without drilling pilot holes if their widest dimension is in the direction of the timber grain, (figure 6.14). Their use in the opposite direction will probably result in splitting, as illustrated. The head of the oval brad, when flush with the timber surface, will not upset the fibres nearly as much as would a wire nail.

Floor brads (figure 6.15) can be driven into timber without the fear of splitting if their widest dimension is also parallel to the timber grain. Although large in section, the blunt end of the brad will tear its way through the fibres, thus making a fairly large hole for itself.

Lost heads can be used as shown in figure 6.16. Its head can

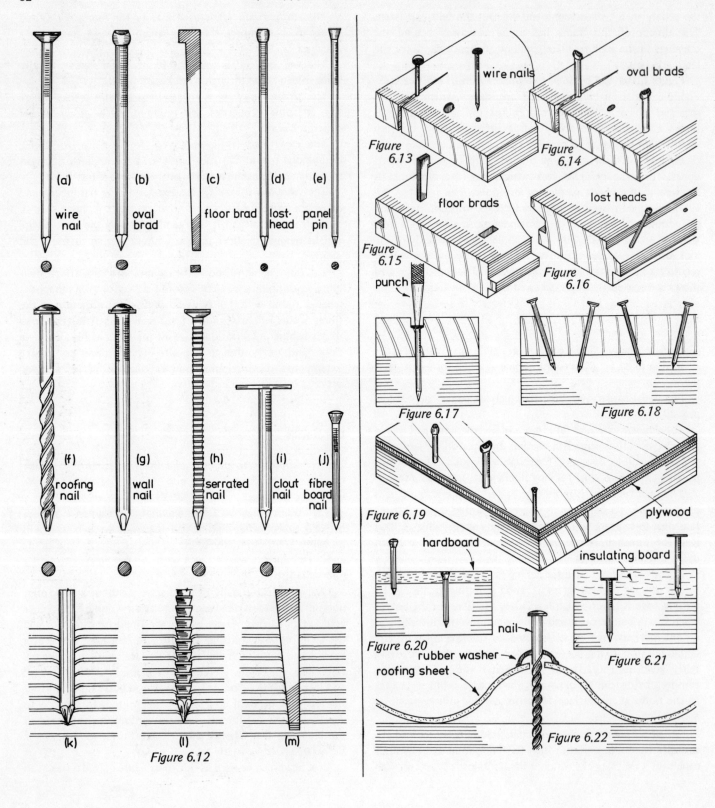

(a) wire nail

(b) oval brad

(c) floor brad

(d) lost-head

(e) panel pin

(f) roofing nail

(g) wall nail

(h) serrated nail

(i) clout nail

(j) fibre board nail

(k)

(l)

(m)

Figure 6.12

wire nails

Figure 6.13

oval brads

Figure 6.14

floor brads

Figure 6.15

lost heads

Figure 6.16

punch

Figure 6.17

Figure 6.18

plywood

Figure 6.19

hardboard

Figure 6.20

insulating board

Figure 6.21

nail

rubber washer

roofing sheet

Figure 6.22

be driven to become flush with the timber's surface, usually without damage.

When nails are used for joinery purposes, it is usual to punch their heads below the surfaces of the timber and to fill the holes (figure 6.17).

Figure 6.18 shows how nailing can be done to obtain extra gripping power. The nails are driven into the timbers in dovetail fashion.

Plywood can usually be nailed to framing without any prior preparation, as shown in figure 6.19.

Oval brads, panel pins, lost heads and similar nails can be used without any fear of splitting.

Fibre-board nails can be used without any splitting occurring and their heads can be driven below the surface due to their shape (figure 6.20).

Insulating boards are often fixed with wide-headed nails, similar to clout nails. If their heads are to be punched below the board surface, dimpling may occur. It is possible to get over this problem by cutting the surface of the board around the nail's head with a hollow punch. The head is then punched home with a nail punch, leaving a flat surface around the opening (figure 6.21).

Figure 6.22 shows a roofing nail fixing a corrugated sheet to roof timbers. To prevent water from getting in through the nail holes, washers, preferably of rubber, must be used below the nail heads.

SCREWS

Figure 6.23a—e shows the types of wood screws in common use.

The *countersunk screw* (a) is used more often than any other screw. Its name is due to the shape of its head. This general purpose screw can be used for almost any work which needs screwing together, but in many instances the appearance of the work is more important and other equally efficient screws must be used.

The *round head screw* (b) is one such screw; it is used on work where it is necessary to keep the screw heads visible, or where the screws may have to be removed from time to time.

The *raised head screw* (c) is used on good-class work where the screws will be visible, such as cabinet work, glazing beads, etc. The head is similar to the countersunk screw, but its top is convex. These screws are usually made from a non-ferrous metal because of the nature of work for which they are used. They are very often used in conjunction with cups, let into the surface of the timber, into which the screw head fits. Their use results in a much neater finish and also helps to maintain high

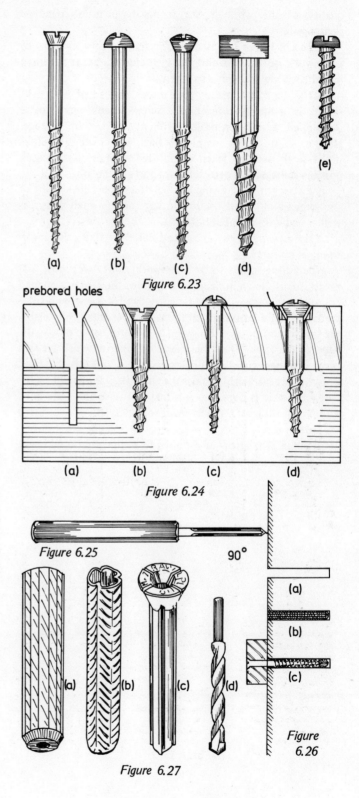

Figure 6.23

Figure 6.24

Figure 6.25

Figure 6.27

Figure 6.26

quality of the work if the screws have to be removed periodically.

A *coach screw* (d) is used for fixing heavy timbers to framework, such as loading bays, platforms, etc. It is turned into the woodwork with a spanner.

To fix timbers together with screws instead of with nails results in a much stronger job. Screws enable work to be dismantled and re-assembled without trouble or damage. Nailing, although not completely final, will create difficulties if the work is to be taken apart after assembly, resulting in possible splitting and destruction of parts of the job.

The strength of screwing can be affected by the spacing of the screws and by the use of too large or too small screws as well as badly drilled pilot holes.

A *self-tapping screw* (e) can be be used for fixing thin metal to metal objects.

When using screws to fix woodwork, *pilot holes* must first be drilled, as shown in figure 6.24. a shows the preparation for a countersunk screw — a hole large enough for the screw to pass through should be drilled in the top timber and a countersink bit should also be used for preparing the timber to receive the head of the screw. The other piece of timber to which the first piece is to be secured should also be drilled, but this hole must only be large enough to take the shank less the width of the thread. If this is done, no splitting will occur and the good gripping qualities of the screw will be preserved.

Three various types of wood screw in position are shown in b, c and d. The arrow at d points to a cup often used below the head of a raised-head screw in good-class work.

Another familiar piece of ironmongery is the *plugging tool*, shown in figure 6.25. It is used to make holes in brickwork or concrete so that wooden objects can be fixed to their surfaces. The tool is struck with a hammer and turned periodically to keep it from jamming in the hole it is drilling. It must be held in the left hand while it is being struck with the hammer and must also be kept at right angles to the wall surface. By striking the tool and turning it continuously a hole will be produced into which a plug can be placed. The screw and object are then placed in position and fixed by turning the screw into the plug in the wall.

Figure 6.26 shows the various stages of fixing a wooden object to a brickwork or similar surface. a shows the hole produced by the tool; its depth should be a little greater than the length of the portion of the screw that will be entering the hole. The plug is pushed into the drilled hole without protruding from it when it is in position (b). The size of the plug should also match that of the plugging tool, which in turn, should match the size of the screws being used. c shows the wooden item fixed by a screw; note that the length of the screw should be such that it does not pass through to the back of the hole.

Figure 6.27a, b and c shows three different types of plug. a is the *common fibre-plug*; b and c are two *non-ferrous metal plugs* suitable for damp situations. d shows a *tipped drill* which is used as an alternative for drilling holes in brickwork.

7. TURNING PIECES AND CENTERS FOR ARCHES

To enable a bricklayer to construct an *arch* over an opening in the wall of **a building**, the carpenter must provide him with a support on which he can lay his bricks to shape the arch. This support can be either a solid piece of timber cut to the shape of the bottom edge of the arch (figure 7.1) — which is called a *turning piece* — or a timber frame as shown in figure 7.2, which is called a *center*. The height of an arch and the thickness of the wall will dictate whether a turning piece or a center is to be provided. Usually, turning pieces are used only for fairly low segmental arches and for flat arches.

Figure 7.3 shows how a segmental arch is set out; a—b is equal to the span of the arch, and c—d is equal to the rise of the arch. The line a—b is called the *springing line.* If a—d is bisected and the bisecting line projected downwards to meet the centre line in e, a compass point can be placed in e and the curve of the arch can be drawn with the radius e—a.

Figure 7.1 shows the elevation of a turning piece suitable for an arch similar to that shown in figure 7.3. It will be noticed that the piece of timber shaped into the turning piece is allowed to extend downwards to below the springing line. This is to prevent the timber finishing to a feather edge at its ends.

Figure 7.4 shows how to draw an isometric view of the turning piece. The base should be divided into any number of equal parts (figure 7.1) and vertical lines drawn up to the top edge from those points.

In the isometric drawing, the base of the turning piece should be drawn at 30° and the points 1, 2, 3, etc., placed on the line. Vertical lines of the same length as in the elevation should be drawn from these points. A freehand curve can be drawn through the points obtained.

The lines that pass across the top edge of the turning piece are drawn at 30° and their lengths are equal to the thickness of the timber used.

Below the turning piece are supporting posts and folding wedges that are used for making final adjustments to the height of the turning piece and to assist in releasing the timbers after the work on the arch has been completed.

Figure 7.5 shows how a centre for a segmental arch is made. Plywood or hardboard lagging is nailed to the top edges of the shaped pieces and the thickness of the lagging must be allowed for when setting out the shape of the ribs. Battens across the lower edges of the shaped ribs keep them in their correct positions.

A center suitable for a semi-circular arch is shown in figure 7.2. Two frames each equal to the shape of the lower edge of the arch are made after deducting (in the setting out) the thickness of the lagging. The frames have shaped ribs built up in two thicknesses, nailed together with the joints staggered. The surfaces of the underneath layer of boards will allow the top ends of the struts to be nailed to them; their lower ends can be nailed to the tie that runs along the lower edges of the frames. The ties and struts are made of single thickness timber.

The frames can be nailed together as shown in figure 7.6, building them up on the full size setting out to ensure that all the timbers are in their correct positions and that they can be cut on the bandsaw to the same circular shape. They should then appear as shown in figure 7.7.

Figure 7.8 shows a vertical section through a semi-circular centre. The braces are nailed to the edges of the struts to keep the centre square across the direction of the thickness of the wall.

Figure 7.9 shows how a flat arch can be constructed. To stop the arch from appearing to sag in the centre, the turning piece is given a slight camber as shown in the diagram. This is usually ignored in the smaller-span arch, since the impression of the sag is only encountered in arches of large span.

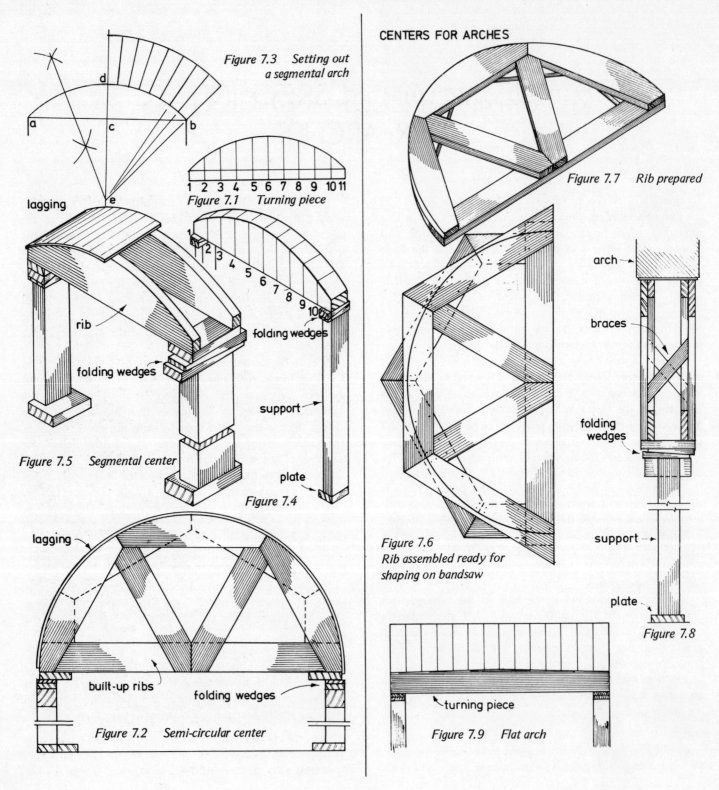

CENTERS FOR ARCHES

Figure 7.3   Setting out a segmental arch

Figure 7.7   Rib prepared

lagging

Figure 7.1   Turning piece

rib

folding wedges

folding wedges

support

Figure 7.5   Segmental center

plate

Figure 7.4

Figure 7.6
Rib assembled ready for shaping on bandsaw

arch

braces

folding wedges

support

plate

Figure 7.8

lagging

built-up ribs

folding wedges

Figure 7.2   Semi-circular center

turning piece

Figure 7.9   Flat arch

8. FORMWORK FOR CONCRETE

Concrete units can be made in two ways: in the factory or any other convenient place and then transported to the site, in which case they are said to be *pre-cast*; or they can be cast on site and in the position for which they are intended. This method is called *in situ casting*.

The formwork can be either solid timber or in sheet form, such as plywood, or it can be made from manufactured mild-steel forms. Timber formwork only will be described in this chapter. Metal formwork will be discussed later in the course.

It is not usual to use good-quality timber for formwork, but the quality of the surface finish of the concrete units can be affected by the kind of timber used. For instance, if the timber is left in its sawn state, the concrete surfaces will be rough. The timber can be planed to give a smooth finish to the concrete or sawn material can be used and the inner surfaces of the timber lined with thin plywood, tempered hardboard or even sheet metal.

The quality of the finish given to the concrete units can also be affected by the tendency of the concrete to adhere to the timber formwork. When this happens, parts of the concrete unit often break off when the formwork is removed. To avoid this, the formwork surfaces can be painted with a liquid known as a *release agent*.

The strength of the timber is important and poor quality timber — which is often used for this type of work — usually has large knots or fairly long splits which tend to weaken it. Where weak timber is used for formwork, additional strength can be provided, if necessary, with extra supports, increased thicknesses of shuttering boards and additional battens to secure these boards, and so on.

Concrete formwork must be designed to be easily adjustable so that, if necessary, final positioning can take place with the minimum of trouble. The concrete jobs described in this section do not require any adjustments to the formwork because the casting boxes can be positioned accurately when the initial fixing takes place. In many concrete jobs which do need adjustments after the work has been erected, *folding wedges* play a large part. Folding wedges are also used in the *striking* of formwork (figure 8.1).

Formwork must also be designed to be removed easily from the concrete and in addition to folding or single wedges, bolts are used for this purpose.

Figure 8.1 shows how to construct the formwork for a single concrete paving slab. Four pieces of reasonably strong timber are used for the sides of the box, say, 50 x 50 mm or 38 x 50 mm, depending on the thickness of slab required. The two longer sides of the box have been recessed to receive the ends of the other pieces and the four pieces are placed on a base which can be made of resin-bonded plywood. Remember not to make the recesses in the sides so that the ends of the short sides will fit tightly in them. Water will enter the timber when the box has been filled resulting in swelling and making it difficult to take the box apart. The thickness of the base board should be at least 12 mm and it should be screwed to battens. The whole job can then be placed on a level surface.

In order to keep the box together while the concrete sets, a batten is screwed to the base near to each of the long sides of the box, allowing enough space between the batten and the box to get in a fairly large wedge. When the concrete has set, the two wedges are tapped free and the box sides are removed.

Figure 8.2 shows a casting box for making three concrete building blocks in one filling. In this case, the two long sides of the box are fairly large timbers. If the block sizes are, say, 450 x 225 x 100 mm, the long sides should be around 100 x 50 mm. Four recesses are made in each of the sides to receive the timbers that will separate the blocks and also form the ends of the box. The whole job can be held together with a bolt at each end as illustrated. The base is well battened to form a strong surface. The thickness of the sides will eliminate the need for a batten and wedge for extra support.

Figure 8.3 shows how a small concrete lintel can be pre-cast. All timbers in this job are fairly thin, say, 25–32 mm. The longest sides of the box have been recessed to receive the

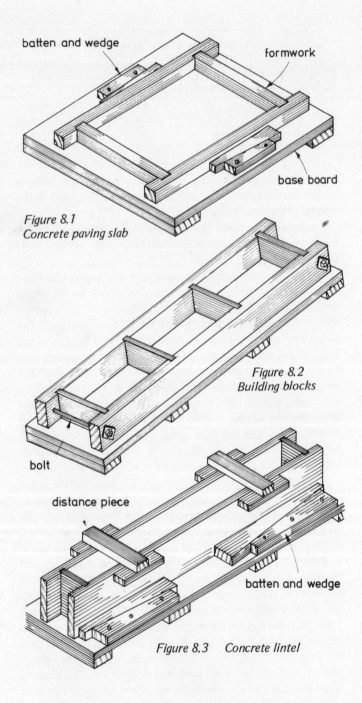

Figure 8.1
Concrete paving slab

Figure 8.2
Building blocks

bolt

distance piece

batten and wedge

Figure 8.3   Concrete lintel

batten and wedge

formwork

base board

CONCRETE FORMWORK-PRECAST UNITS

ends of the short sides. The box rests on a base board and is held in position at its lower edges with battens and wedges in the same way as shown in figure 8.1. The top of the box can be supported with distance pieces that can easily be removed when the concrete has set.

Before filling with concrete check that the boxes are square and tap them into true squares with a hammer if necessary.

Figure 8.4 shows an isometric view of a concrete sundial--stand or bird table. It consists of three sections — the lower part or base, the centre portion or *stem* and the top. The base and the top can be made in a similar way to the slab shown in figure 8.1. If only one of these items is to be made, the four pieces of timber can be used for both sections, the base being made first and the four pieces recut to form the smaller slab. If several are to be made, then sets of timber for the base and for the top sections will be required (figure 8.5).

The elevation of the formwork for the stem is shown in figure 8.6. Two tapered pieces as shown are required, the taper in the other direction can be obtained by cutting the two ends of the box to different lengths. The sides of the box can be held together with bolts, two bolts at each end being advisable. Distance pieces across the top with battens and wedges along the lower edges will help to keep the box firmly in position.

In the space below the elevation make a drawing of the plan of the casting box.

IN SITU WORK

Simple examples of *in situ* castings of concrete are shown in figures 8.7, 8.8 and 8.9. Figure 8.7 shows how a concrete path can be cast in sections. All that is required when the position for the path has been cleared and a thin layer of hardcore laid and consolidated, are strips of wood to form the box and some pegs to hold the box sides in position while the concrete is poured and allowed to harden.

The box sides must be positioned with the aid of a spirit level to ensure a level pathway and a constant width of path — a strip of wood equal to the width should be prepared so that the sides are parallel.

Figure 8.8 shows how a small concrete ramp can be cast at the side of a doorway or opening in a building to be used for easy access for loaded barrows, trucks, etc. In this case, the concrete must not be allowed to taper off to a very thin edge; to provide for an edge of, say, 75 mm thickness at the ramp's lowest end, the ground should be excavated to a depth of 150 mm, and 75 mm of hardcore laid in the bottom of the excavation and consolidated.

The formwork consists of two tapered pieces of timber,

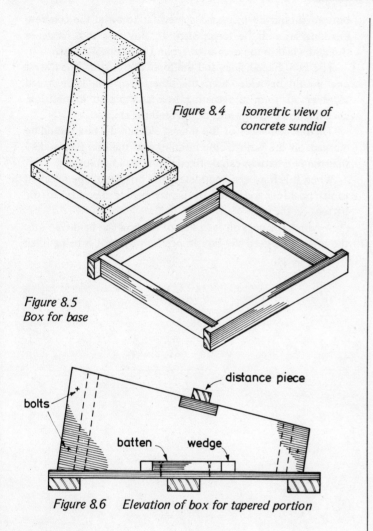

Figure 8.4   Isometric view of concrete sundial

Figure 8.5
Box for base

Figure 8.6   Elevation of box for tapered portion

bolts

distance piece

batten   wedge

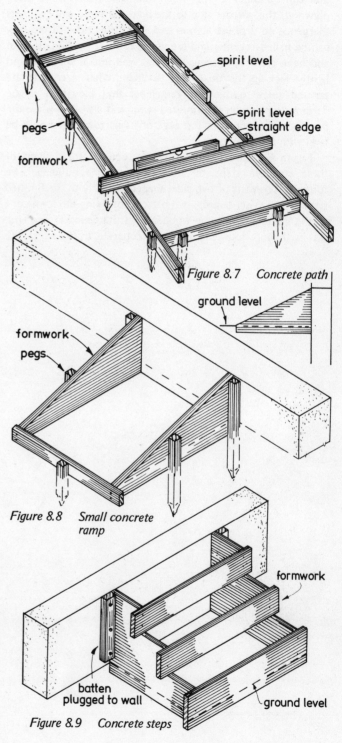

spirit level

spirit level
straight edge

pegs

formwork

Figure 8.7   Concrete path

ground level

formwork

pegs

Figure 8.8   Small concrete ramp

formwork

batten
plugged to wall

ground level

Figure 8.9   Concrete steps

that can be either 25 mm thick solid timber or 12 mm thick plywood, the narrow side to the box and some wooden pegs sharpened to a point at one end. The three sides of the box can be nailed together and the whole can be placed in position and held there by driving the pegs well into the ground and lightly tacking the box sides to them. When preparing the tapered sides to the box, remember that they have to be 75 mm deeper than the finished ramp and also that when the box is in position, the top edge of its narrow side should be level with the ground.

Figure 8.9 shows the formwork required for a flight of three concrete steps to allow access to a building. The formwork consists of two sides shaped similarly to the finished steps — three riser boards, two battens for fixing the formwork to the building and some wooden pegs sharpened at one end. As in the previous example, the concrete thickness at the bottom should be increased somewhat to avoid the concrete breaking around the lower step. In this case too, hardcore should be laid in the excavated ground and consolidated.

The two shaped sides and the three riser boards (the lowest one should be wider than the other two) should be nailed together to form the casting box and placed in position, checking the overall width of the required steps.

The outside edges of the shaped sides of the box should be marked on the walls of the building and the box removed so that the two battens can be fixed to the wall by plugging.

When this has been completed, the box should be returned to its position and fixed by lightly nailing the sides to the battens on the wall.

A couple of pegs on each side of the box can be driven into the ground to keep the box in position while it is being filled with concrete.

9. GROUND FLOORS

Great care must be taken in the construction of timber floors, especially of *suspended ground-floors*, because serious problems may arise in a building at this point. Badly-constructed ground floors are often the cause of *dry rot* attacking the timbers in a building. The omission of damp-proof courses, inadequate ventilation underneath the floors, timbers built in or touching the outer brick walls are common causes of trouble. It is essential to prevent the absorption of moisture by timbers forming part of a building because if a certain water level is reached, namely, 20 per cent of the dry weight of the timber, and if other conditions also prevail, then dry rot will occur.

Additional conditions that favour an attack of dry rot are
(i) warm atmosphere
(ii) lack of light
(iii) food, such as starches and sugars, contained in the timbers.

These factors, along with moisture and lack of ventilation, provide ideal conditions for an attack of the fungi causing dry rot.

The subject of dry rot and its eradication has been dealt with in chapter 1, but the methods of constructing a ground floor designed to prevent an attack must be emphasised here.

Figures 9.1 and 9.2 show the corner of a suspended timber ground-floor. The term 'suspended' is applied to this type of floor because of the space below the timbers.

The dimensions of the timber joists in this floor are usually around 100 x 50 mm. They are not deep enough to span any great length, hence walls (called *sleeper walls*) are constructed at intervals of approximately 1.75 m centres across the width of the span, as illustrated in figure 9.3. The sleeper walls have to be constructed with openings in the brickwork (figure 9.4) to allow an adequate supply of fresh air to pass over the lower surfaces of the timbers to assist in the evaporation of the moisture in the space and on the timber surfaces. The fresh air enters the space below the floor through the air bricks that are built into and around the main walls of the building just above ground level, as seen in the illustration.

On top of each of the honeycombed sleeper-walls is placed

a *damp-proof course* (usually a bituminous and asbestos compound) to prevent any moisture rising up through the walls into the timbers. On top of the damp-proof course (d.p.c.) are placed *wall plates* to which the joists are fixed.

Not only the sleeper walls, but also all the other walls throughout the building must have damp-proof courses. Those in the main wall are also shown in figure 9.1. Note also that no timber in the floor is in contact with the main walls of the building, nor do any of the sleeper walls come into contact with the main walls. All these points help to eliminate moisture from the timbers.

The construction of a timber floor around a fireplace opening presents one or two problems, such as the supporting of the floor joists adjacent to the hearth and the construction of the concrete hearth, in which the carpenter plays his part.

Figure 9.5 shows a plan of the timbers around a fireplace in a suspended ground-floor. The minimum projection of the concrete hearth in front of the fireplace opening is 500 mm; this is indicated in figures 9.5 and 9.6. A *fender wall* is built to support the timbers in front of the fireplace and also to contain the hearth. This is a brick wall that extends outwards from the centres of the chimney breasts so that the wall plate, which supports the joists in front of the fireplace, is at least 500 mm from the fireplace opening. This fender wall must have a damp-proof course like all the other walls in the building.

On top of the front section of the wall is placed a wall plate to which the timber joists are fixed. To enable the concrete hearth to be made, a three sided box, with its top surface flush with the floor joists, is made to the required hearth-dimensions and fitted centrally in front of the fireplace. This box will remain in position after the hearth and floor have been constructed and its two side pieces will be used for fixing the floor boards at each side of the hearth.

Hardcore is then laid in the bottom of the void made by the fender wall up to a level that will allow a 100 mm thick concrete hearth to be laid with its top surface flush with the sides of the box.

The floor joists can now be laid after the plates have been

GROUND FLOOR CONSTRUCTION

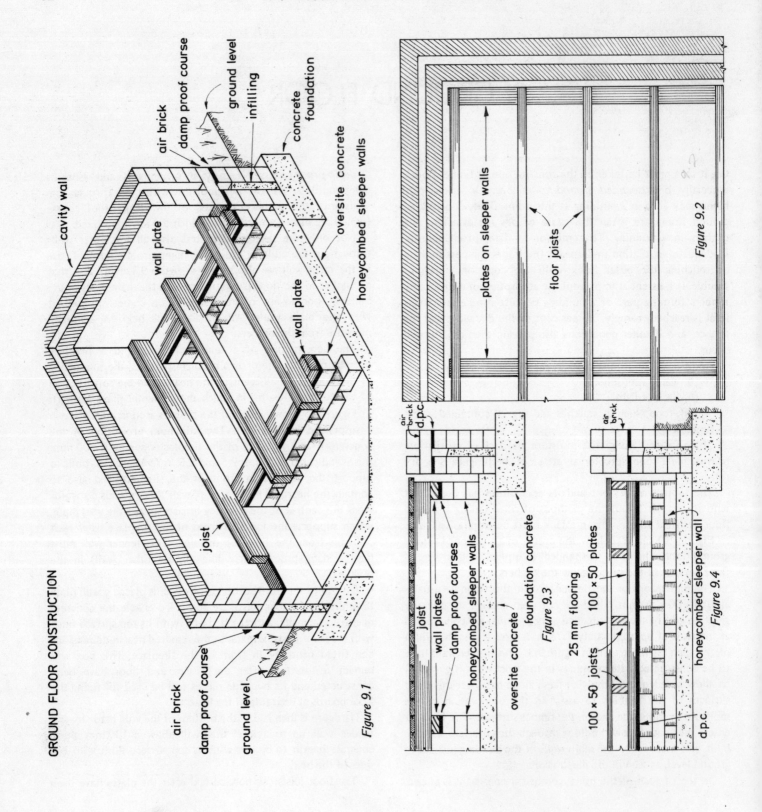

cavity wall

air brick
damp proof course
ground level
infilling
concrete foundation

wall plate

oversite concrete

wall plate

honeycombed sleeper walls

joist

air brick
damp proof course
ground level

Figure 9.1

plates on sleeper walls

floor joists

Figure 9.2

air brick
d.p.c.

joist
wall plates
damp proof courses
honeycombed sleeper walls
oversite concrete
foundation concrete

Figure 9.3

air brick

25 mm flooring
100 × 50 plates
100 × 50 joists
d.p.c.
honeycombed sleeper wall

Figure 9.4

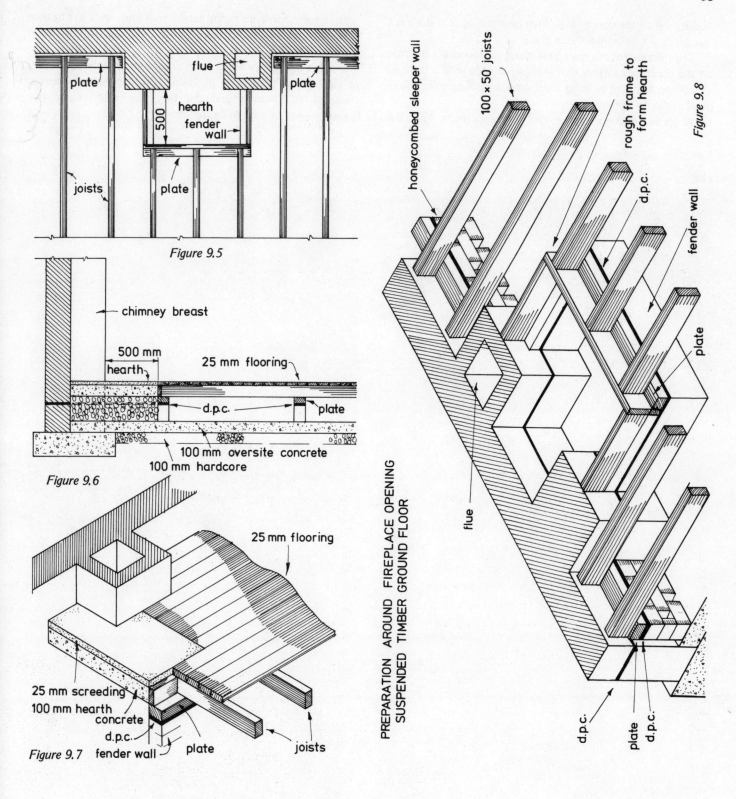

plate

flue

plate

500

hearth
fender
wall

joists

plate

Figure 9.5

chimney breast

500 mm

hearth

25 mm flooring

d.p.c.

plate

100 mm oversite concrete

100 mm hardcore

Figure 9.6

25 mm flooring

25 mm screeding

100 mm hearth
concrete

d.p.c.

fender wall

plate

joists

Figure 9.7

honeycombed sleeper wall

100 × 50 joists

rough frame to
form hearth

d.p.c.

fender wall

flue

plate

d.p.c.

plate

d.p.c.

Figure 9.8

PREPARATION AROUND FIREPLACE OPENING
SUSPENDED TIMBER GROUND FLOOR

bedded on to the sleeper walls, first ascertaining that there is a damp-proof course under each plate.

The floorboards can then be laid and cut round the position of the concrete hearth which is then screeded with a mixture of cement and sand to bring the finished hearth up to the same level as the floorboards.

A vertical section through the floor appears in figure 9.6 showing the hardcore in the fender-wall area, with the hearth concrete and cement screeding above and flush with the floor surface.

Figure 9.7 shows the timbers around the fireplace. Finally, a view of all timbers in position — the damp-proof courses inserted in all walls and the box that will include the hearth — may be seen in figure 9.8.

10. ROOFS

Roofs can be categorised as single roofs or double roofs. Single roofs — to which this chapter is devoted — do not require intermediate supports to their rafters.

The span of the building on which the roof rests determines whether or not the rafters will require additional supports, because the size of the rafters increases as the distance between the main walls widens. As a general rule, if a rafter is longer than 2.25 m it should receive an additional support near its centre. However, many modern roofs are constructed entirely of *roof trusses* which will be covered at a later stage. (Roof trusses are frames made to the shape of the roof and so constructed that no further supporting timbers are needed.)

The cost of timber and the lack of adequate supplies makes it necessary to conserve timber by using smaller-size timbers and reinforcing them. A short time ago it was common practice to use 100 x 50 mm timbers for roof work, but now, due mainly to cost and developments in design, smaller timbers in the region of 75 x 50 mm to 75 x 25 mm are used.

Figure 10.1 shows a cross-section through a *lean-to roof*. A wall plate has been bedded on to the top of the outer wall with a lime—cement—sand mortar and a wall piece has been fixed with plugs and screws to the wall of the building against which the roof is to rest.

The *pitch* of the roof is the angle of the sloping surface (figure 10.2) — 45° in this case. The rafters are cut to fit against the wall piece at the top and are notched to fit over the top outside corner of the wall plate at their lower ends. They are securely nailed to the plate and wall piece with 100 mm wire nails and are allowed to run down beyond the wall plate so that the eaves can be finished as required.

In this case the rafters are cut off flush with the outside face of the wall and a *fascia board*, to which the *gutter* is fixed, is nailed securely to the ends of the rafters. The rafters should be spaced along the length of the roof at approximately 400 mm centres. Provided that the rafters are not longer than 2.25 m, they will not need the addition of a *purlin*, which is the name given to the additional support previously mentioned.

It may be required to construct a ceiling in the space below the lean-to roof and details of this are shown by broken lines. Another wall piece to take one end of the ceiling joists must be fixed to the face of the wall of the main building and the joists notched into this. Their other ends are allowed to rest on the wall plate and can be securely nailed to the rafters and the plates, again using 100 mm wire nails.

If small timbers are used and it is considered that they are inadequate to resist the weight of the ceiling material (for instance, plasterboard) it will be necessary to run a *binder* over the centres of the ceiling joists to which they can all be nailed. The binder can be given support by nailing vertical pieces of timber at, say, 1.5 m centres along its length, to the rafters of the roof and notching them around the binder and securely nailing to the lower timbers.

A *couple roof* (figure 10.3) is a pitched roof having a span not greater than 2.5 m if no ceiling is needed in the space below. However, if a ceiling is required, then the roof becomes a *couple close roof* (figure 10.4) which can have a span of up to 4 m.

Figure 10.5 shows a *collar roof*, which is similar to a couple close roof, but in this case the ceiling rafters are raised to provide more head room in the building.

The joint between the collars and the rafters must be adequate and a bolted joint with a timber connector between the timbers is advisable. The distance at which the collars are fitted above the normal ceiling-rafter position must not be greater than one-third of the height of the roof.

Figure 10.6 shows a small couple roof, suitable for a garage. It has gabled ends with an overhang of the roof at the ends. The illustration shows how these ends are constructed. The wall plates and the ridge are allowed to pass beyond the end walls so that the overhanging rafters can be fixed in position. Other timbers, fixed to the rafters within the building, are allowed to cantilever outwards to give additional support to the overhanging rafters.

In figure 10.6, the various parts of the roof have been lettered. In the spaces below give each its correct name

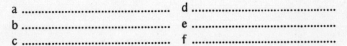

a .... d ....

b .... e ....

c .... f ....

The *eaves* of a roof are the lower edges of the sloping surfaces. Figure 10.7 shows flush eaves, which are very seldom used these days other than for lean-to roofs. There are several ways of finishing the eaves.

Figure 10.8 shows details of open eaves, although the sprocket piece is not a part of open eaves; it is merely an addition and can be used on any type of roof, if so desired.

Open eaves merely means that the rafters have been allowed to run past the face of the wall and cut off to any desired shape, usually to that shown in the illustration. The gutter is often held in position on such a roof by purpose-made brackets which are screwed on the sides of the rafters. Figure 10.9 shows details of closed eaves. Rough brackets fixed to the feet of the rafter allow a soffit board to be fixed and a fascia board fixed to the front of the rafters to support the gutter.

Simple roofs such as gable and lean-to roofs require little marking out. All that is required is the development of the length of the common rafters.

Figure 10.10 shows a section through a lean-to roof; the problem here is to mark out the length of a common rafter so that it can be prepared and then used as a templet to mark out the remainder. As can be seen in the illustrations, the effective span is the horizontal distance between the face of the wall of the main building and the outside surface of the wall plate. The rafter comes to this point at the required angle or pitch and then extends farther so that the required finish to the eaves can be obtained. In this example, the horizontal distance of the overhang is indicated by x.

To mark out the first common rafter.

(i) Measure carefully the horizontal distance between the wall and the outside edge of the wall plate.

(ii) Draw, to a scale of 1:10, a right-angled triangle, similar to that shown in figure 10.11, making x equal to the horizontal distance between wall and wall plate and the sloping line y — a equal to the pitch of the roof.

(iii) Measure the line y — a carefully with the scale rule and multiply this dimension x10. This will be the true length of the rafter from the wall to the top outside corner of the wall plate.

(iv) Take the piece of timber to be marked out and draw a line along its length, parallel to its lower edge and one-third the depth of the timber away from this edge. All measurements must be made along this line.

(v) Set up two sliding bevels, the first to the bevel or

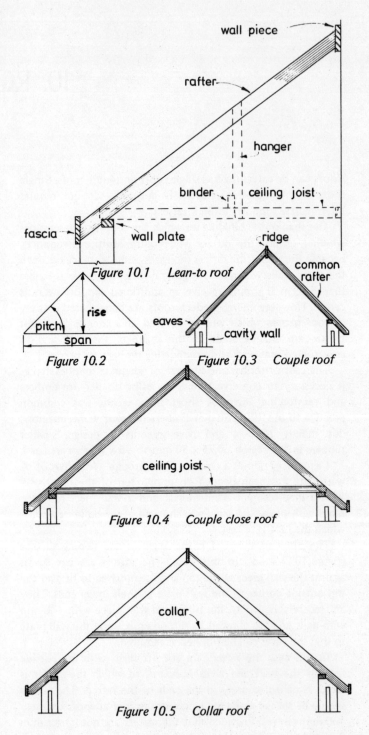

Figure 10.1   Lean-to roof

Figure 10.2

Figure 10.3   Couple roof

Figure 10.4   Couple close roof

Figure 10.5   Collar roof

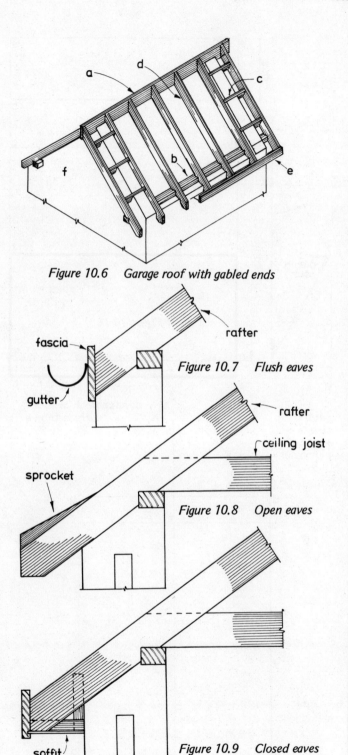

Figure 10.6   Garage roof with gabled ends

Figure 10.7   Flush eaves

Figure 10.8   Open eaves

Figure 10.9   Closed eaves

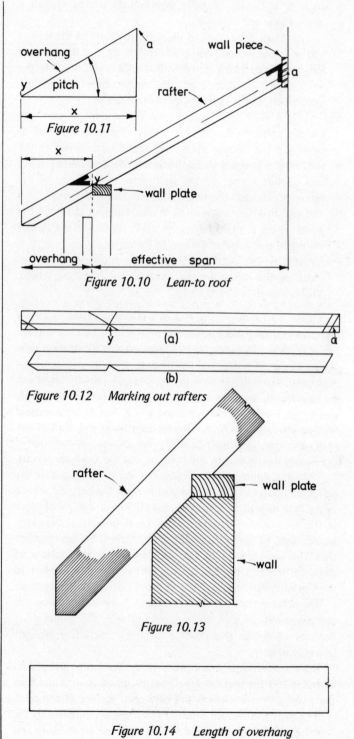

Figure 10.11

Figure 10.10   Lean-to roof

Figure 10.12   Marking out rafters

Figure 10.13

Figure 10.14   Length of overhang

angle 'a' at the top of the triangle and the second to angle y at the lower end of a — y.

(vi) Mark the angle a at the right-hand end of the timber and with the second sliding bevel mark angle y, the distance they are apart being equal to that of a — y. Complete the marking of the notching by using the first bevel through the same point, but at right angles to the angle y.

(vii) Figure 10.11 shows how the amount of overhang for the rafters is found; this is very similar to the method described for finding the length of the rafter down to the notching. x is equal to the horizontal distance between the top outside corner of the wall plate and the end of the rafter. Construct the triangle and measure the side a — y and add this dimension on to the marking out to obtain the point where the two bevels are again applied to the timber to obtain the shape at the end of the rafter.

(viii) Before cutting the rafter, the thickness of the wall piece at the top end must be deducted from the length. This is shown in figure 10.12.

Figure 10.13 shows the end of a common rafter to a roof and the end of a piece of timber which is to be used for the rafter is shown in figure 10.14. Show on this illustration how the piece should be marked out prior to shaping.

Figure 10.15 shows how the surfaces of a pitched roof can be developed. a — b — c — d is the plan of the roof, a — b — f — e is the elevation and a — d — e shows a vertical section through the roof. The section shows the span of the roof, the rise and the pitch. It also shows the two bevels previously mentioned in the marking out for the lean-to roof.

This is a double pitched roof, but the marking out of the rafters is similar to that of the lean-to roof, the only difference being that instead of deducting the thickness of the wall piece at the tops of the rafters, the thickness of half of the ridge board must be deducted in this case. It must be remembered that the span shown in the roof section is the horizontal distance between the top outside corner of one wall plate to the top outside corner of that at the opposite side of the roof.

To develop one of the surfaces of the roof, place the compass point in e in the section and with the radius e — a describe an arc to give point a' on the vertical line brought down from e.

Draw a horizontal line from a' in the section to give points a' and b' on the vertical lines brought down from a and b in the plan. a' — b' — f — e is the developed surface of the roof.

The plan and section through a roof appear in figure 10.16. Develop one of its surfaces and with a protractor measure and write down, in the spaces provided, the number of degrees in the pitch, seat and plumb cuts and measure the rise and

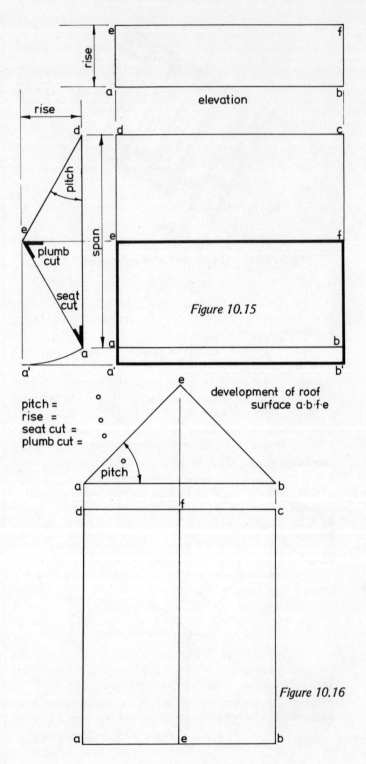

Figure 10.15

pitch = ○
rise = ○
seat cut = ○
plumb cut =

development of roof surface a·b·f·e

Figure 10.16

11. DOORS AND FRAMES

Ledged-and-braced doors and frames are used for various purposes outside the house, such as for the back entrance to a garage, for shed and outhouse doors. They are comparatively easy to construct and it is usually not necessary to use a setting-out rod.

The main panel of the door consists of a series of boards, usually matchboarding, held together with battens. Braces are included in the construction to prevent the door from sagging on the side farthest from the hinges — hence the importance of their position in the door.

Figure 11.1a shows a rear elevation of a ledged-and-braced door in a frame. The boards should be so positioned that the two edge boards are of the same width. This is important when matchboarding is being used in order to avoid having a narrow strip on one of the edges of the door. (Figures 11.1b and c show vertical and horizontal sections of the door and frame.)

Three ledges or battens are used for holding the boards together; they are nailed through the face of the boards, using nails long enough to penetrate through the battens at the back to an extent of, say, 10 mm, so that their ends can be *clenched*. The method used for clenching is shown in figures 11.2a–d. First the heads of the wire nails should be flattened on a piece of metal so that large holes will not be made in the face of the boards. The heads should then be punched well into the surface of the boards. The door is then turned over and the nails clenched — in other words, bent over and their ends punched into the surface of the battens.

Two braces are also shown in the illustrations; they are notched into the edges of the battens and fixed in the same way. The direction of the braces must be as indicated in the illustration, namely, their lower ends should be nearest to the side of the door on which the hinges are fixed.

When the door frame is made, it should have some temporary braces nailed to its top corners and a distance piece secured near to the lower end to keep it in its correct shape as it is built into the brickwork (figure 11.3). The joints at the top of the frame are simple mortice and tenons, glued with a resin adhesive and draw bored (figure 11.4).

The door frame is placed in position as the brickwork is being laid and is held in a vertical position by means of a piece of timber which is nailed to the top of the frame and fixed at the bottom by bricks, as seen in figure 11.5. In this type of external frame, a metal dowel is often let into the lower end of each jamb of the frame and is allowed to enter a hole cut in the concrete floor and later grouted in with cement and sand grouting, as indicated in figure 11.1a.

As the brickwork is brought up towards the top of the frame, metal clamps are screwed on to its sides and built into the brickwork as the building proceeds (figure 11.6).

Care must be taken to position the frame correctly in the vertical position and to do this a plumb rule or spirit level should be used, as shown in figure 11.5.

Figure 11.7 gives an indication of how much the brace should be let into the ledges.

Figures 11.8–11.11 show various items of ironmongery used for the ledged-and-braced doors.

The tower bolt (figure 11.8) and the barrel bolt (figure 11.9) are used for keeping the door bolted from the inside. Two bolts should be fixed to each door; the most convenient places to fix them are at the ends of the top and bottom ledges. The Norfolk latch (figure 11.10) is used for keeping the door securely closed, part a being fixed to the outside of the door and part b to the inside. Figure 11.11 shows the type of hinge used for hanging ledged-and-braced doors.

The timber-cutting list below relates to the door frame. Insert the missing figures in the list for a door 2 m long by 0.8 m wide.

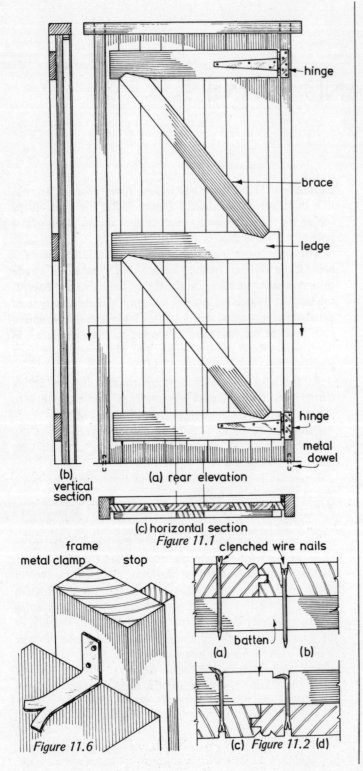

hinge

brace

ledge

hinge

metal
dowel

(b)
vertical
section

(a) rear elevation

(c) horizontal section
Figure 11.1

frame
metal clamp   stop

Figure 11.6

clenched wire nails

batten

(a)   (b)

(c)   Figure 11.2 (d)

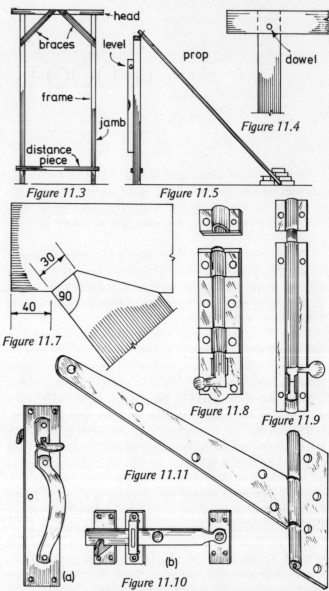

head

braces   level   prop

frame   dowel

jamb

distance
piece

Figure 11.3   Figure 11.5   Figure 11.4

30

40   90

Figure 11.7

Figure 11.8   Figure 11.9

Figure 11.11

(a)   Figure 11.10   (b)

TIMBER CUTTING LIST				
	ITEM	N°	SAWN SIZES	FINISHED S.
DOOR FRAME	JAMBS	2	× 100 × 50	95 × 45
	HEAD	1	× 100 × 50	95 × 45

12. SINGLE-LIGHT CASEMENT-WINDOWS

Windows are designed to admit light and air into buildings; they can be hinged, in which case they are termed *casement windows*; when they are made to pivot around a centre point, they are called *pivot-hung sashes* and windows designed to slide in a vertical or horizontal direction are described as *sliding sashes* or *boxed frames with sliding sashes.*

Casement widows consist of an outer frame and one or more glazed inner frames, called casements, which can be hinged to the outer frame. The casements are occasionally fixed in the outer frame. The frame and casements (without the glass) are fixed in position by means of galvanized-metal cramps screwed to the outer frame. Before leaving the factory for the building site, the whole assembly should be given at least two coats of pink primer.

Windows should be designed to be weatherproof. To achieve this aim, windows should have *mortar grooves* around the outside edges of the outer frame; reasonably good joints between the outer frame and the casement; a good slope on the top outer surface of the *cill*; a *drip groove* on the outer lower surface of the cill; a *waterbar groove* (or mortar groove) also on the cill's lower surface, and *anti-capillary grooves* around the rebates of the outer frame and lower surface of the bottom rail to the casement.

Figure 12.1 shows the elevation of a simple, single-light casement-window. The outer frame consists of two *jambs* — the name given to the side members; the head at the top, and the cill at the bottom. The inner frame, which is the casement, consists of two side members called *stiles*, a *top rail* and a *bottom rail.*

Figure 12.2 shows a section through a jamb of the frame and a stile of the casement. Note that the *rebate* for the glass is placed to the outside of the window. The mortar groove in the frame should, if possible, be positioned to miss the mortice and tenon joints at the corners of the frame.

Figure 12.3 shows a section through the cill of the frame and the bottom rail of the casement. The cills to casement windows are bevelled and are very often slightly wider than the other members of the frame. This helps to shed any water that would tend to dampen and stain the surrounding brickwork.

Before making a casement window, the work has to be set out; this means that a workshop rod has to be made to enable a cutting list to be prepared and to enable the marker-out to place the various lines on the pieces of timber which comprise the job.

Figure 12.4 illustrates a workshop rod for a simple casement window. It must be set out, full size, on a sheet of plywood, a narrow strip of prepared board or on a piece of paper. Timber is generally the best material for rods because paper can shrink or expand due to changes in atmospheric moisture, but paper is more suitable in certain cases.

A rod must contain sufficient information to enable the work to be carried out without having to refer to any other source of information. It must show the overall dimensions of the job, the finished sizes of the components as well as their shapes and positions in the work. Vertical and horizontal full-size sections are often sufficient for making out a workshop rod, but this depends on the job in hand. Sometimes it is necessary to make two or more horizontal sections instead of the usual one, if the details are different at various heights and this also applies to vertical sections for the same reason.

Figure 12.4 shows a vertical and a horizontal section through the casement window shown in figure 12.1. Only one section of each is required in this case because there is no change in construction between the two jambs of the frame or between the head and cill. The overall height and the overall width have been indicated on the rod and when drawing the two full-size sections, it must be remembered that the components must be drawn to their finished sizes and not to their stock or sawn sizes. For instance, if the sawn sizes for the jambs of the frame are 100 x 75 mm, an allowance must be made for the preparation of the material by machine — hence the finished sizes would measure say, 95 x 70 mm. The jambs must be drawn in the horizontal section to these finished sizes, that is 95 x 70 mm. This applies to all other pieces — the head, the cill and those making up the casement. At least 5 mm must be deducted both from the width and the thickness of each piece to allow for machining. Some firms allow more than 5 mm and their rules in this respect must be carried out. Remember too, that stock-size timbers must always be used as far as possible for economy.

After completing the workshop rod, a cutting list should be compiled giving sawn and finished sizes. The timber is then obtained from the store and sent to the machine shop.

An incomplete cutting list for the casement and frame appears below. Fill in the missing figures.

Item	No. required	Sawn sizes	Finished sizes
Jamb	2	1000 x 100 x 75	95 x 70
Head		670 x x	95 x
Cill	1	670 x 125 x 75	x 70
Stile		950 x 50 x 50	x
Top rail	1	560 x x	45 x 45
Bottom rail	1	x 75 x	x

Figures 12.5—12.7 show the usual types of ironmongery used with casement windows.

The casement fastener (see figure 12.5) is used for fixing the window in the closed position; the striking plate shown in a is used when the window opens outwards and that shown in b is fixed to the inside surface of a jamb when the window opens inwards. The Parliament hinge (figure 12.6) and similar hinges are used where the casement is required to be thrown well clear of the frame when the window is opened to enable the outside surfaces of the glass to be cleaned, but butt hinges are frequently used for hanging casements. Figure 12.7 shows a casement stay which enables the window to be fixed in the open position.

When the rod, cutting list and timber have been prepared, the next job is the marking out. This means that the various lines have to be placed on the pieces of timber to allow the joiner or machinist to prepare each piece before the whole job is assembled.

Marking out for the joiner differs considerably from marking out for the machinist. This difference will be explained in the following paragraphs in respect of a simple job such as a single casement and frame.

Let us take another casement and frame, the workshop rod of which is shown in figure 12.8. We shall first deal with the marking out for the joiner.

The face marks are first placed on all pieces and then the marking out proceeds. The jambs for the frame should be marked out as a pair (figure 12.9) and to be certain of this, the

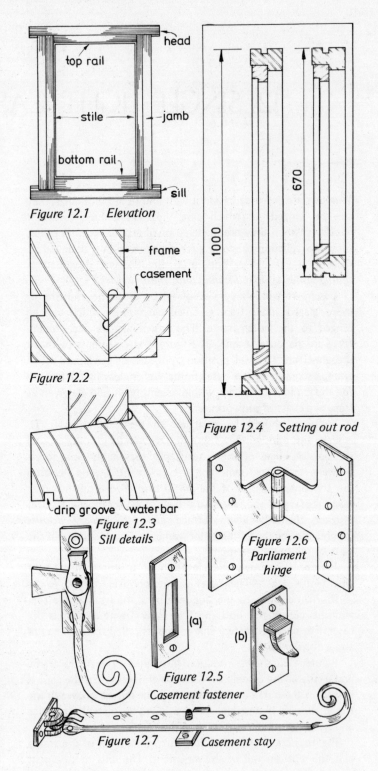

Figure 12.1   Elevation

Figure 12.2

Figure 12.3
Sill details

drip groove   waterbar

Figure 12.4   Setting out rod

Figure 12.6
Parliament
hinge

Figure 12.5
Casement fastener

(a)

(b)

Figure 12.7   Casement stay

face mark on one piece should be facing the front and that on the second piece should be facing the rear.

First mark the sight lines with a pencil on the inside edges of the pieces and the shoulder lines, which should be made with a marking knife and squared all round each piece. The positions of the sight and shoulder lines are obtained by placing one of the pieces on the setting-out rod and marking from the vertical section. The two jamb pieces are then placed together on the bench and the points squared over to the second piece. The positions of the tenons, rebates, mouldings and grooves should also be placed on each piece. These can be marked either with a mortice gauge or a marking gauge.

The same procedure is followed for the marking out of the other pieces that form the frame. The head and cill are both placed on the rod and the positions of the mortices are then marked with a mortice gauge, having first selected the appropriate mortice chisel and setting up the mortice gauge to this size. After this has been done, the remaining marks can be placed on the timber, such as the mouldings, rebates, grooves, etc. The marking out of the cill is shown in figure 12.10. Remember, the marking out lines on the pieces of timber should all be marked from the face side or face edge. This will help to avoid mistakes in marking out and ensure that various mouldings, grooves, etc. will line up correctly in the finished job.

It will be noticed that the shapes of the finished sections have been drawn on the edges of all the pieces. They are sketched quickly by the marker-out to enable the joiner to see at a glance what each piece should look like when it is ready for assembly. Figures 12.11, 12.12 and 12.13 show how the stiles, top rail and bottom rail of the casement are marked out prior to shaping.

Explain briefly the procedure in placing the various pencil, cut and gauge lines on each of these pieces.

Which lines should be marked with a knife? ....
....

Which lines should be marked with a pencil? ....
....

Which lines should be marked with a mortice gauge? ....
....

Which lines should be marked with a marking gauge? ....
....

The marking out of the casement components should be as

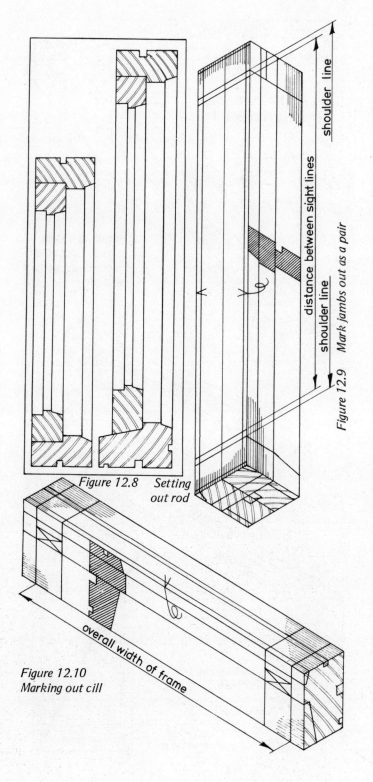

Figure 12.8   Setting out rod

Figure 12.9   Mark jambs out as a pair

shoulder line

distance between sight lines

shoulder line

Figure 12.10
Marking out cill

overall width of frame

follows

....

....

....

....

When all marking out has been completed, the various parts are shaped ready for assembly. It is usual to cut the mortices first and then the tenons, fitting the first tenon to be cut to one of the prepared mortices to make certain that the lines denoting the thickness of the tenon are correct, or, in the case of the tenons being cut on a tenoning machine, to make certain that the machine has been set up correctly for the tenon cutting and that the scribing at the shoulders is correct.

After the mortices and tenons have been cut, the rebating, moulding and the grooving can be done to complete the work of shaping.

The two frames are then assembled and any fitting, such as the scribing of the shoulders, can be done. When taken apart the inside surfaces are cleaned off and the frames glued and finished off ready for priming. While the gluing is carried out, check that the work is square, using a squaring rod (figure 12.14).

Now we come to the marking out of components for the machinist.

Figure 12.15 shows the marking out for the jambs. Only one piece of timber is required because once the tenon has been set up for one jamb, any number can be cut to this size. It is only necessary to make a note on the piece telling the machinist that so many pairs 'at this' are required. The sawn size is also given on the piece. No sight lines are shown; shoulder lines are positioned, but in contrast to the joiner's requirements, only pencil lines are needed. The distance between the shoulder lines is marked on the edge of the jamb piece.

Tenons are denoted by drawing two lines as opposed to one line to denote mortices, as seen in figures 12.15 and 12.17.

The positions of the tenons are given to the machinist by printing a note near to one of the positions telling him the size and position, in mm, from the face edge. In this case the note says: '19 mm T (tenon) 32 mm ON' ('32 mm ON' means 32 mm from the face edge).

A section has also to be drawn on the timber (figure 12.16) to show its finished shape and notes must be placed around the section explaining the sizes and positions of each rebate, groove, etc.

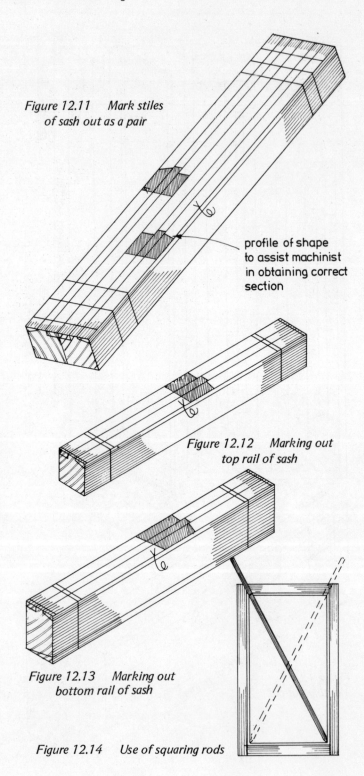

Figure 12.11   Mark stiles of sash out as a pair

profile of shape to assist machinist in obtaining correct section

Figure 12.12   Marking out top rail of sash

Figure 12.13   Marking out bottom rail of sash

Figure 12.14   Use of squaring rods

MARKING OUT FOR THE MACHINIST

STORMPROOF CASEMENT WINDOWS

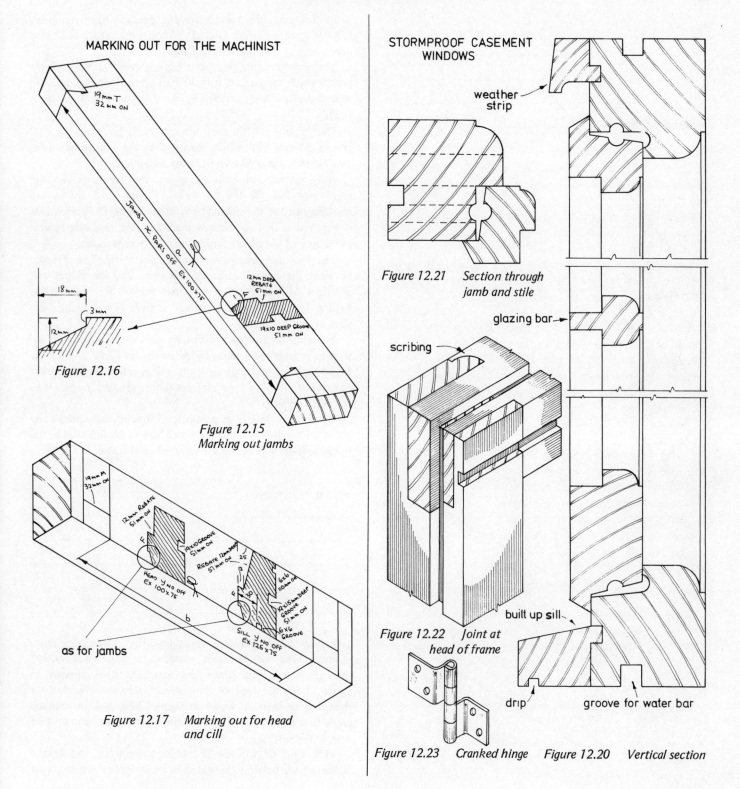

Figure 12.16

Figure 12.15
Marking out jambs

Figure 12.17   Marking out for head and cill

weather strip

Figure 12.21   Section through jamb and stile

glazing bar

scribing

Figure 12.22   Joint at head of frame

built up sill

drip

groove for water bar

Figure 12.23   Cranked hinge

Figure 12.20   Vertical section

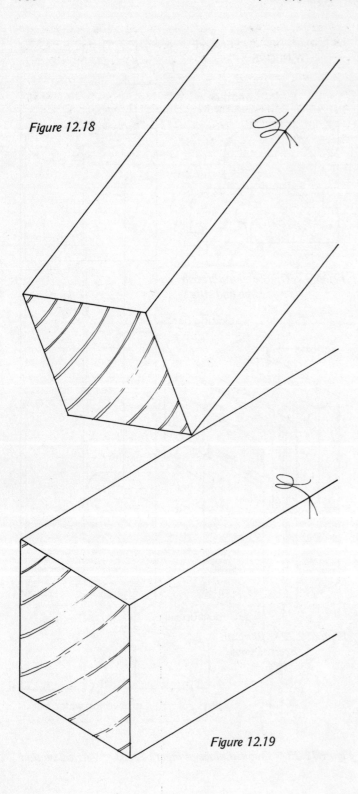

Figure 12.18

Figure 12.19

In this case, the rebate size and position has been given (12 mm rebate 51 mm ON). This means the rebate is 12 mm deep and is 51 mm from the face edge.

The moulding on the front edge is given as '18 x 12 x 3 bevel' which means that it is situated on the face edge and the overall depth of the moulding is 18 x 12 mm with a 3 mm deep sinking.

The groove on the bottom surface is given as '19 x 10 groove 51 mm ON' which means that the groove measures 19 x 10 mm and is 51 mm from the face edge.

Also marked on the piece are the scribings for the mouldings and for the cill bevel. Figure 12.17 shows the marking out for the cill and head to the frame. Only one piece is required with two sections placed on the face side to give the shapes of the pieces, which are of different width.

The mortices are shown by one line only. The distance between the jambs or mortices is given and the shapes and positions of mouldings, grooves and rebates are indicated as before. The number of pieces 'off' is given as well as the sawn sizes of the components.

The ends of the top and bottom rails of the casements are shown in large-scale illustrations in figures 12.18 and 12.19. Insert on these drawings the various lines and notes the marker out would place on their surfaces before sending the pieces to the machine shop.

Describe, as briefly as possible, all the necessary marks and notes on the timbers and the procedure to be followed in the machine shop to produce the casement and frame.

....

....

....

....

....

....

Figure 12.20 shows a vertical section through a more modern type of casement window; a horizontal section through one of its jambs and casement stiles appears in figure 12.21; the type of joint which is commonly used for this kind of work is shown in figure 12.22, and the cranked hinge that must be used to allow the casement to open may be seen in figure 12.23.

This kind of window is termed *stormproof* and several features have been incorporated in its design to ensure, as far as possible, that it lives up to this name. For instance, the head of the frame has a weather fillet tongued and grooved to its front surface, its function is to throw any water (which would otherwise run down the window) well clear of the woodwork. The face of the casement comes out beyond the face of the frame allowing rebates to be worked on its outside edges which overlap the edges of the rebate, thus helping to exclude water and draughts. Large joints are allowed in this construction because of this lipping and large capillary grooves are worked on the edges of the casement and on the surfaces of the rebates, which also tend to prevent water and draughts entering the building. The cill has been built up. This will save a considerable amount of timber in its preparation. Note that the pivot point for opening the window must be at the outside edge of the lipping on the hinge side of the casement stile. A wide joint also is necessary at the opposite side of the casement to allow for its opening.

13. SHELVING

The type of *shelving* and *shelf support* to be used is often determined by the weights that are to be placed on it and by its location. For example, shelves for books in a library would normally be specified to be of higher grade than shelves for books kept in a storeroom.

Shelves that have to support heavy loads such as machinery, must be strong enough to withstand not merely rough treatment but also possible overloading; additional strength properties are therefore important.

One of several methods used for producing such shelving (and its supports) is shown in figure 13.1. The shelf consists of slats or battens – the dimensions of which depend on the items to be stored – spaced across the width of *gallows brackets*. These brackets consist of two pieces of timber connected with a dovetailed joint; they are held at right angles by a strut notched into their inside surfaces. The three pieces are glued and screwed together, thus making a very strong bracket capable of withstanding heavy loads provided it is correctly connected to the wall. This can be done in several ways; for example, the brackets can be plugged to the wall with fibre plugs (for example Rawlplugs), using fairly large screws and plugs (No. 12 or 14) or, if this fixing method is not considered to be adequate, the use of rawlbolts is recommended.

Figure 13.2 shows another view of this type of bracket and shelving. The mild-steel bracket illustrated in figure 13.3 is used only in medium-priced jobs, such as shelving in garages, store rooms, or in the home where the appearance of the job is not very important and the weight to be supported is not very great. The best way to fix this type of bracket is to fix battens to the wall with rawlplugs and screws to which the metal brackets can then be screwed with wood screws (usually roundheads).

Figure 13.4 shows another view of this type of bracket. Solid boards, 19 mm thick say, provide the shelves which are fixed to these brackets with short round-headed screws. Figures 13.5 and 13.6 show the plugging tool and type of plug to use for fixing the battens to the walls.

Figure 13.7 illustrates an alloy shelf-bracket for good-class work. This bracket (a short end of a tee section) has a ragged-end which is built into the wall, protruding sufficiently to finish just short, or flush with, the edge of the shelf it is to support. To make a neat job, the ends of the shelf have to be fitted to the bracket, as indicated in the illustration. If the end of the bracket is kept back from the front edge of the shelf, the bracket will be hidden from view when the work has been completed.

Figure 13.8 shows another method of supporting shelves, which is often used for bookcases and library shelving. Two narrow strips with a series of slots are recessed into the sides of the bookcase. Into these slots are inserted *metal nibs* (shown near the bottom of the drawing) at the height at which the shelf is to be positioned. Two more strips at the other end of the casing, with the nibs inserted, will support the shelving.

The method, illustrated in figure 13.9, is similar to that just described: *notched battens* are glued and screwed to the casing in the vertical direction and battens are cut to fit into the notches of the vertical supports. The ends of the shelf have to be shaped to fit between the vertical pieces so they can be supported by the battens.

The advantage of these two types of shelving is that the shelving can be adjusted as required.

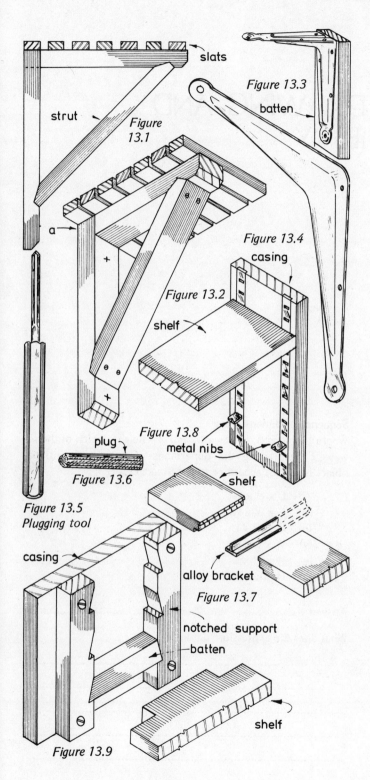

slats

Figure 13.3

batten

strut

Figure 13.1

a

Figure 13.4

casing

Figure 13.2

shelf

Figure 13.8

metal nibs

plug

Figure 13.6

shelf

Figure 13.5
Plugging tool

casing

alloy bracket

Figure 13.7

notched support

batten

shelf

Figure 13.9

14. TECHNICAL DRAWING AND GEOMETRY

DRAWING-OFFICE PRACTICE (BS 1192: 1969 — METRIC)

All building drawings should be produced according to the Drawing-office Practice booklet, published by the British Standards Institution (BS 1192: 1969 — Metric). Students should acquaint themselves with this publication which stipulates the accepted rules for all building drawings. Deviation from these recommended rules can lead to confusion.

Insert in the spaces below the preferred scales for the following types of drawing

Type	Preferred scales (metric)
Block plan	
Site plan	
Location (such as ground-floor plan of house)	
Component drawings	
Details	
Assembly	

Dimension Lines

There are several separate dimension lines for figured dimensions and their termination denotes the type of dimension each represents.

Draw below several lines to represent dimension lines, with the various types of termination, as indicated in BS 1192, and add notes stating to which it refers.

Sequence of dimensioning

Where L = length, W = width and H = height, which of the six ways of expressing the dimensions of a three-dimensional object is correct according to the Standard?

- (i)   L x H x W
- (ii) L x W x H
- (iii) H x W x L
- (iv) W x L x H
- (v)   W x H x L
- (vi) H x L x W

Answer ....
....

What does the expression 'datum' mean?

....

....

....

....

....

....

How should existing levels and intended levels be expressed?

(i) Existing level ....

(ii) Intended level ....

Lettering on drawings

What is the object of lettering on drawings?

....

....

Should lettering on drawings be underlined? ....

Should punctuation marks be used on drawings?

....

....

How can uniform letters and numerals be produced on a drawing?

....

....

What are the recommended sizes for letters and numerals?

....

Orthographic projection

Orthographic projection makes it possible to give details of an object by drawing a number of different views of the object, such as a plan, an elevation, etc.

What is the recommended style of orthographic projection for building drawings?

....

What other conventional style is available?

....

How does it differ from the recommended style?

....

....

....

....

Graphic symbols

Write down or sketch the symbol recommended for the following

Centre to centre	Centre line ....
Direction of view	External ....
Internal	Bench mark ....
Finished floor line	Ground level ....
Hectare	Kilometre ....
Metre	Millimetre ....

Representation of materials

Materials are indicated on drawings according to recommended methods. Make drawings of these recommendations against each of the materials named below

Brick	Concrete
Earth	Fibre board
Glass	Hard core
Loose insulation	Partition block
Plywood	Screed

Stone   Wood (Unwrot)

Wood (Wrot)

What is the meaning of the terms *Wrot* and *Unwrot*?

....

....

....

....

....

BUILDING DRAWINGS

Basic requirements

Instrument	Use
Metric scale rule	
45° Set square	
30°/60° Set square	
Compasses	
Dividers	
Protractor	
Soft rubber	
Pencils	
Drawing board	
Tee square	
Clips or drawing pins	

Drawing boards and tee squares are usually supplied by Technical Colleges.

Buy good quality instruments.

Keep pencil and compass leads in good order — a chisel point is best.

Protect your instruments at all times.

Occasionally wash your set squares with soapy water.

Have a soft pencil for lettering and a medium-hard pencil for drawing. Avoid rubbing out as much as possible.

When purchasing a scale rule, make sure that it includes the following scales — 1:1, 1:5, 1:10, 1:20 and 1:50. You must master the use of your metric scale rule. Figure 14.1 shows one end of a scale rule and also shows how to extract dimensions from it. In addition to working the problems out at the bottom of the page, draw the following lines, using the scale indicated, 50 mm (1:5); 1 m (1:20); 250 mm (1:10); 750 mm (1:5).

Compasses and dividers (figure 14.2) are essential for drawings and are used for many purposes apart from drawing circles.

Compasses are used for

1. Drawing circles.

2. ....

3. ....

4. ....

Dividers are used for

1. Transferring dimensions from one drawing to another.

2. ....

3. ....

If good and reasonably expensive compasses and dividers are purchased, spares can be obtained to replace worn out or broken parts. Explain briefly the purposes of the various parts labelled in the drawings in figure 14.2.

a. Is a circular nut for securing the steel point in the compass.

b. ....

....

c. ....

....

d. ....

....

e. ....

....

f. ....

....

g. ....

....

What is the name of the instrument shown on the right of the dividers? ....

What is its main purpose? ....

....

THE METRIC SCALE RULE

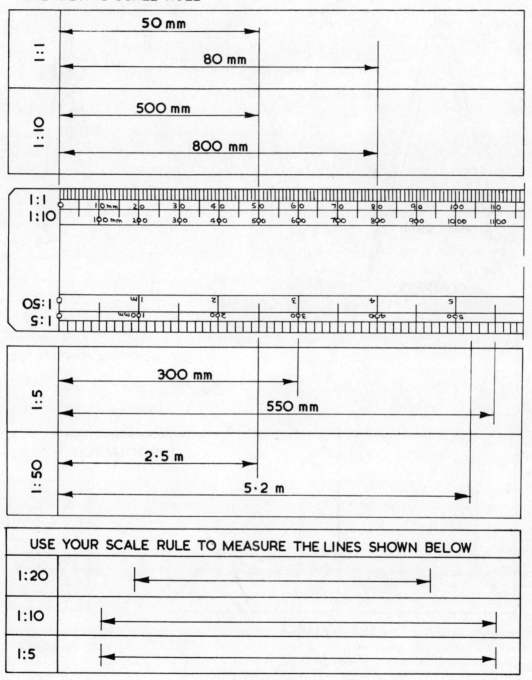

Figure 14.1

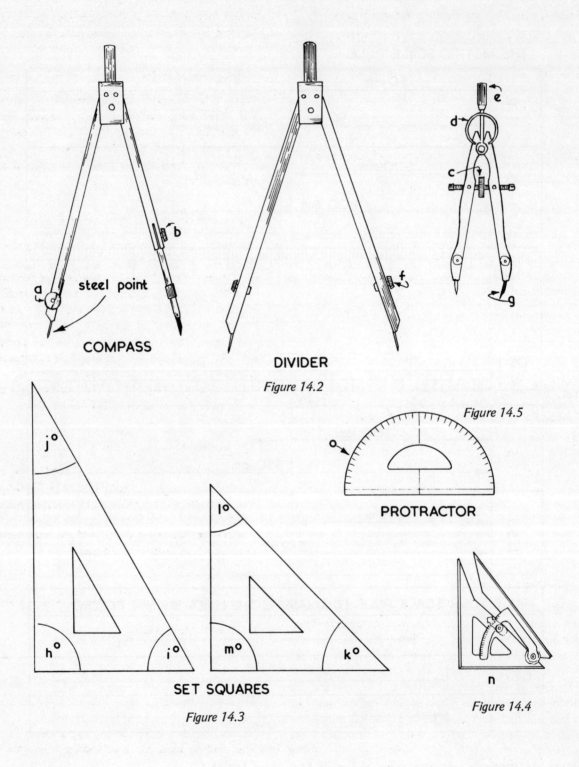

COMPASS

DIVIDER

Figure 14.2

Figure 14.5

PROTRACTOR

SET SQUARES

Figure 14.3

Figure 14.4

Set squares (figure 14.3) are usually purchased in pairs.

What are the numbers of degrees in the corners of the set squares shown?

h = 90°   i = ...

j = ...   k = ...

l = ...   m = ...

What is the name of the instrument shown in figure 14.4?

....

What makes it more useful than other similar instruments?

....

....

Another instrument is shown in figure 14.5.

What is its purpose?

....

....

If drawing pins are used for fixing drawing paper to drawing boards over a long period the surface of the board will become pitted with holes, thus spoiling its efficiency. Pins should never be used — make a sketch of an alternative in the space below.

Setting out drawing paper

Most colleges and drawing offices in large firms who produce their own detailed drawings have their own particular methods for preparing a drawing sheet prior to the production of a working drawing. Most methods usually specify a border all round with a panel either across the bottom of the sheet or placed in one of the bottom corners. The relevant job information is entered in this panel. In colleges the information will include the student's name, his course and year, date, sheet number and the title and sub-title of the lesson.

When placing lettering on drawings, two faint guide lines should first be drawn on the paper with the tee square to keep lettering in a straight line and to keep the sheet neat and tidy.

Construction of angles

Many different angles can be drawn by using the tee square and either one or both of the set squares. Some of these combinations are shown in figure 14.6. One set square is a 45° square and the other is a 30°/60° square.

Work out the indicated angles and write the answers in the spaces provided.

Construction of angles with compasses

Compasses can also be used for constructing some angles such as 90°, 45°, 60°, and 30°.

A right angle (figure 14.7) is drawn by placing the compass in c, drawing the semi-circle and then placing the compass in each end of the semi-circle to obtain the intersecting arcs above. The angles a — c — e and b — c — e are right angles. The 45° angle (figure 14.8) is obtained by bisecting a right angle. The 60° angle (figure 14.9) is drawn by constructing the arc to any radius and then marking the radius from b.

Construct the angle of 30° on the line a — b at the bottom of the page (below figure 14.11).

The protractor

The protractor, when correctly used, can assist in the construction of any angle. Figure 14.10 shows how this instrument is used. Figure 14.11 shows a protractor over the line a — b.

Construct the angles of 15° and 75° indicated below on the two lines at the bottom of the page.

What is an acute angle?

....

What is an obtuse angle?

....

The scale of chords

Yet another device for constructing angles is a scale of chords. The method used for constructing this scale is shown in figure 14.12.

ANGLES

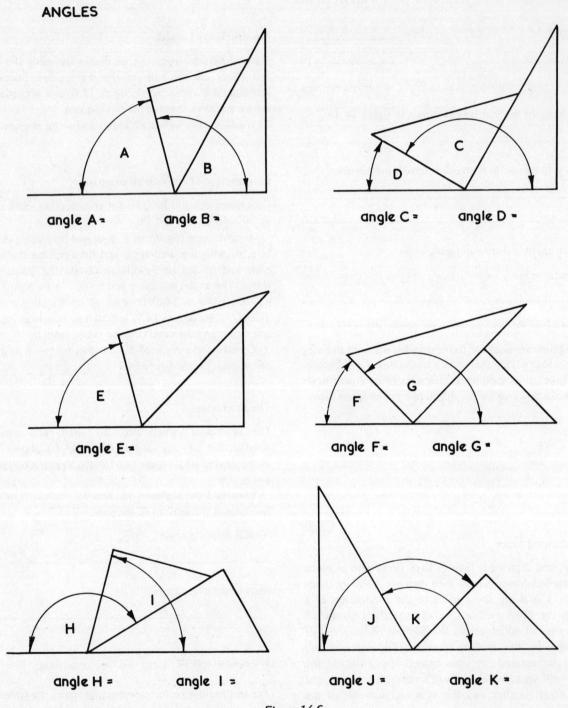

angle A =   angle B =

angle C =   angle D =

angle E =

angle F =   angle G =

angle H =   angle I =

angle J =   angle K =

Figure 14.6

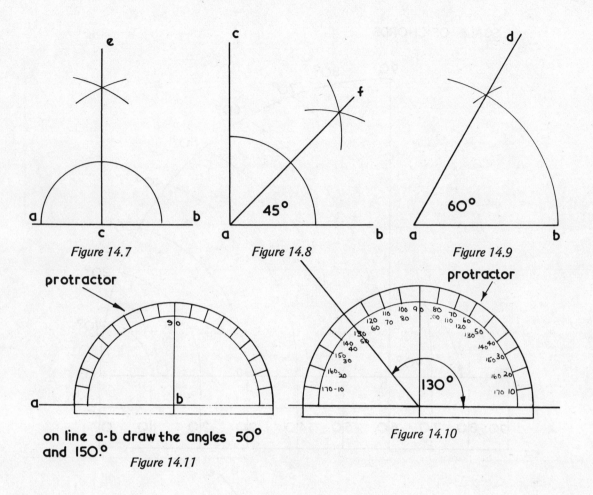

Figure 14.7

Figure 14.8

Figure 14.9

protractor

protractor

on line a-b draw the angles 50°
and 150.°

Figure 14.11

Figure 14.10

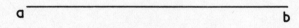

construct an angle of 30°
on the line a-b.

draw the angles of 15° and 75° on the lines
a-b above using a protractor.

SCALE OF CHORDS

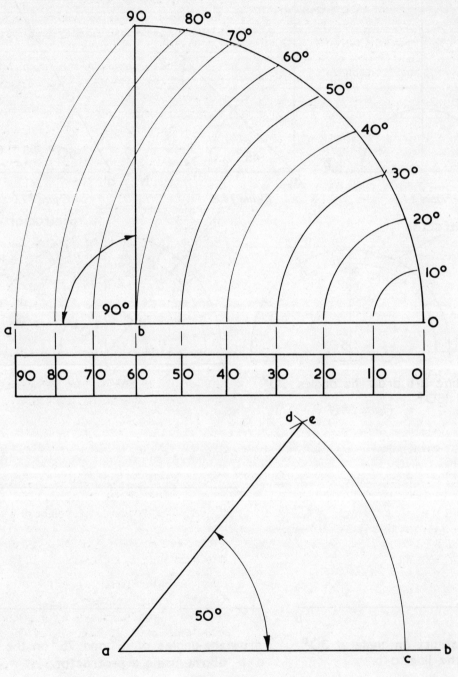

Figure 14.12

First draw the horizontal line a — o and then open your compasses to any radius to describe the quadrant and then draw the vertical line from where the compass point was placed (b) to obtain the 90° line. Then mark on the curve the points 30° and 60° (by the same method as previously shown) and then divide the spaces 0—30°, 30°—60° and 60°—90° exactly into three equal parts to give 10°, 20°, etc. Then with the compass point in 0°, swing arcs from all points on the curve down to the horizontal line. Then construct the scale of chords below as shown in the drawings.

Suppose an angle of 50° is required. Draw line a — b and with the compass point in a and radius 0—60° (always this radius for any angle) draw the arc c — d. Then with compass open 0 — 50° (from the scale) mark off this distance from c to give point e. Draw the line a — e to give the required angle.

A scale of chords, which can be made from a strip of plywood, is useful in a workshop for setting out awkward angles.

Representing objects in drawings

Pictorial projections

Isometric (Figure 14.13) No surfaces are seen in true elevation. Horizontal lines are drawn at 30°. Vertical lines remain vertical. Considered best for pictorial sketches.

Oblique (Figure 14.14) Front surface seen in true elevation. Horizontal lines passing from front to back are drawn at 45°. Vertical lines remain vertical. Not considered good — object always looks out of proportion.

Orthographic projections

1st Angle (Figure 14.15) Front elevation above plan. Side elevation showing the left-hand side surface is placed on the right of the front elevation.

3rd Angle (Figure 14.16) Plan placed above front elevation. Left-hand side of surface shown on the left of the front elevation.

Combination of 1st and 3rd angle (Figure 14.17) Plan below front elevation. Left-hand side elevation placed on the left-hand side of the front elevation.

Type of Projection	Used for
Isometric	
Oblique	
1st Angle	
3rd Angle	
1st and 3rd Angle	

Isometric pictorial projections

This is the most popular method of pictorial representation of an object. Vertical lines remain vertical in isometric drawings. Horizontal lines are drawn at 30°. Inclined lines cannot be drawn directly on to an isometric drawing (measure along horizontal and/or vertical lines to obtain correct positions of inclined lines).

It is often necessary to draw the plan and elevation of an object before an isometric view can be drawn.

Figure 14.18 shows a plan and elevation and isometric drawing of a simple wedge.

Look at the drawings of the folding wedges. (Figures 14.19 and 14.20). In this case the plan or the elevation can be drawn first. Later it will be found that either one or the other must be drawn first to enable the second to be prepared.

Figure 14.21 shows a plan and elevation of a simple dovetailed joint. The isometric view should be completed by the student.

Figure 14.22 shows the elevation and isometric view of a semi-circle. The line 0 — 8 in the illustration is drawn at 30° and the vertical lines are made to coincide with those in the elevation.

Figure 14.23 shows the plan and elevation of a segmental turning piece, below which is a pictorial view to be completed by the student.

Figure 14.24 shows a plan and elevation and isometric view of a corner halving joint.

Figure 14.25 shows a plan and elevation of a dovetailed halving joint. The isometric view should be completed by the student.

Quadrilaterals

A figure with four straight sides is called a quadrilateral. There are six in all illustrated in figure 14.26a—f. a is a square; b a rectangle; c a rhombus; d a rhomboid; e a trapezoid and f a trapezium.

To construct any one of these figures, sufficient information must be given, for instance

Square — length of sides;
Rectangle — length and height;
Rhombus — length of one side and size of one angle;
Rhomboid — length of base, size of one angle and vertical height;
Trapezoid — length of two parallel sides, angles at base, and vertical height;
Trapezium — length of four sides, angles between sides.

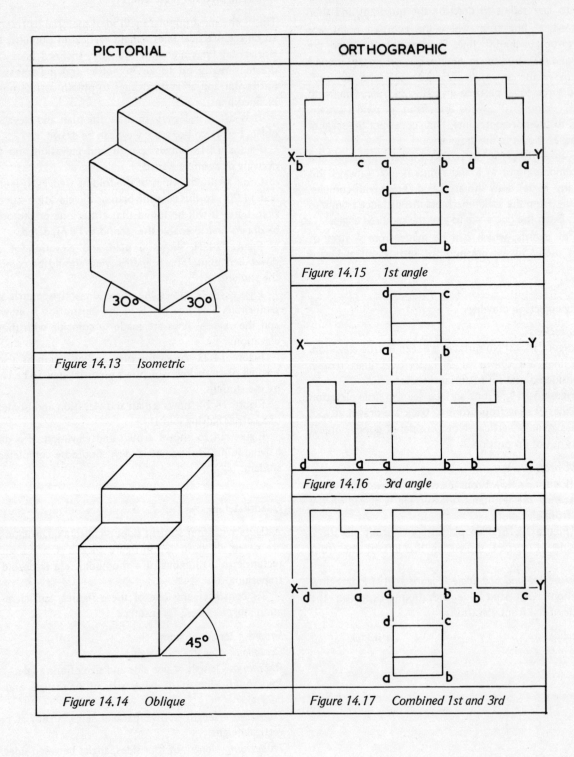

PICTORIAL

Figure 14.13   Isometric

30°   30°

45°

Figure 14.14   Oblique

ORTHOGRAPHIC

Figure 14.15   1st angle

Figure 14.16   3rd angle

Figure 14.17   Combined 1st and 3rd

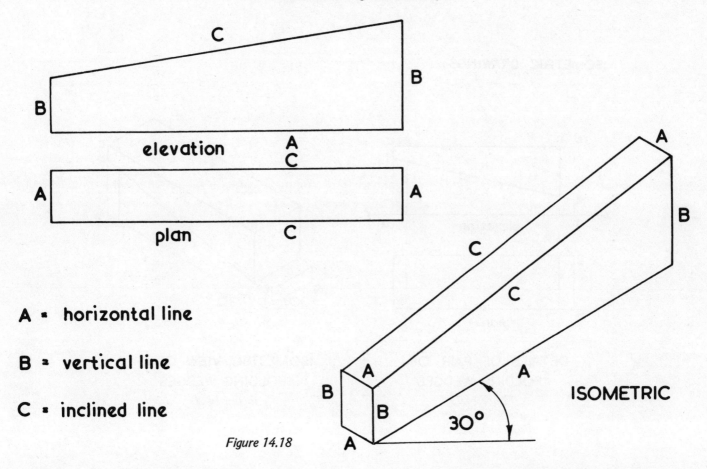

C

B

elevation

A

A

plan C

A = horizontal line

B = vertical line

C = inclined line

A

B

C

C

A

B

B

A

30°

ISOMETRIC

Figure 14.18

Each of the six quadrilaterals has its own definition. Sufficient of these definitions have been included below for the drawings in figure 14.26. Place in the spaces provided the names of the appropriate quadrilateral.

Triangles

There are four types of triangle (figure 14.27). What are their names?

(a) .... (c) ....

(b) .... (d) ....

Which side of which triangle is called the hypotenuse?

....

How many degrees are there in the three angles of any triangle?

....

A triangle containing an angle of 90° has two of its sides equal in length. How many degrees are in each of the two remaining angles?
(i) .... (ii) ....

The formula $a^2 + b^2 = c^2$ can be applied to a triangle. Which triangle? ....

What does the above formula mean?
Give at least two examples in building work in which the formula can be applied.
If $a^2 = 9$ and $b^2 = 16$ how long is the third side of a triangle to which this formula can be applied?

Areas of quadrilaterals

Figure 14.28 shows how to draw a square equal in area to a rectangle abcd. Draw quadrant c − h from centre b. Bisect a − h in j. Draw semi-circle with radius j − h, extend b − c to f; b − f is one side of the square.

ISOMETRIC DRAWINGS

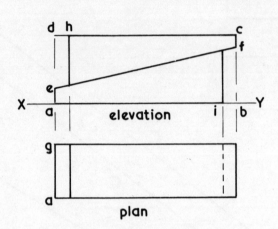

**DETAILS OF PAIR OF
FOLDING WEDGES**
Figure 14.19

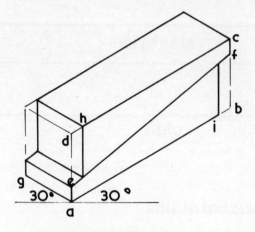

**ISOMETRIC VIEW OF
FOLDING WEDGES**
Figure 14.20

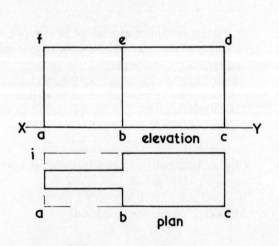

RAIL WITH TENON

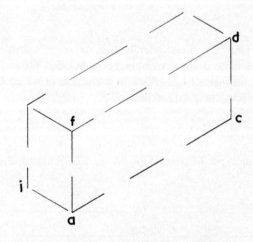

**COMPLETE THE ISOMETRIC
VIEW OF RAIL WITH TENON**

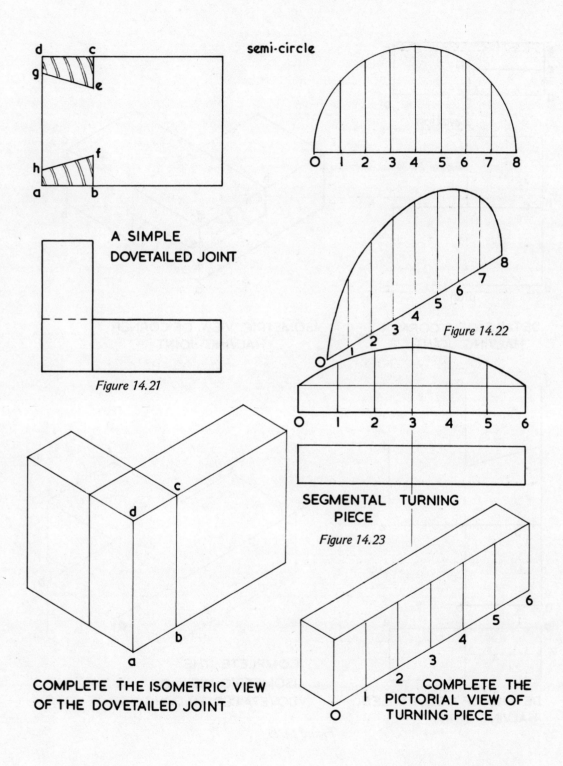

semi-circle

A SIMPLE
DOVETAILED JOINT

Figure 14.21

Figure 14.22

SEGMENTAL TURNING
PIECE

Figure 14.23

COMPLETE THE ISOMETRIC VIEW
OF THE DOVETAILED JOINT

COMPLETE THE
PICTORIAL VIEW OF
TURNING PIECE

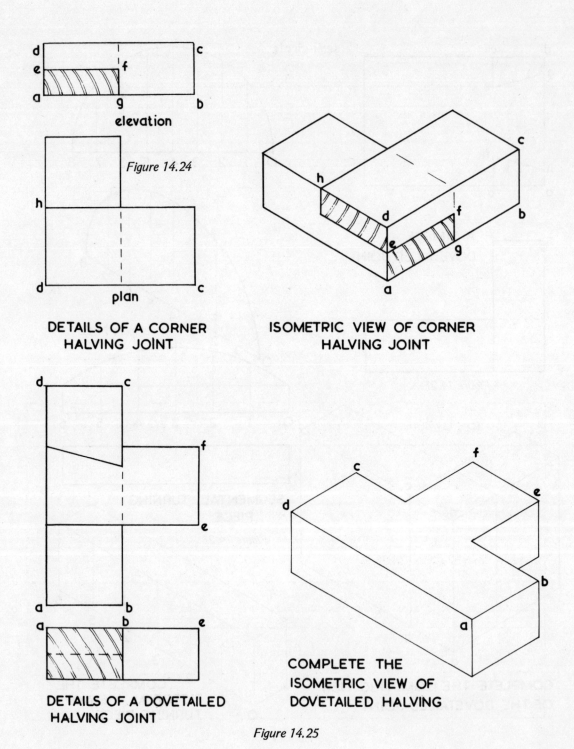

elevation

Figure 14.24

plan

DETAILS OF A CORNER
HALVING JOINT

ISOMETRIC VIEW OF CORNER
HALVING JOINT

DETAILS OF A DOVETAILED
HALVING JOINT

COMPLETE THE
ISOMETRIC VIEW OF
DOVETAILED HALVING

Figure 14.25

QUADRILATERALS

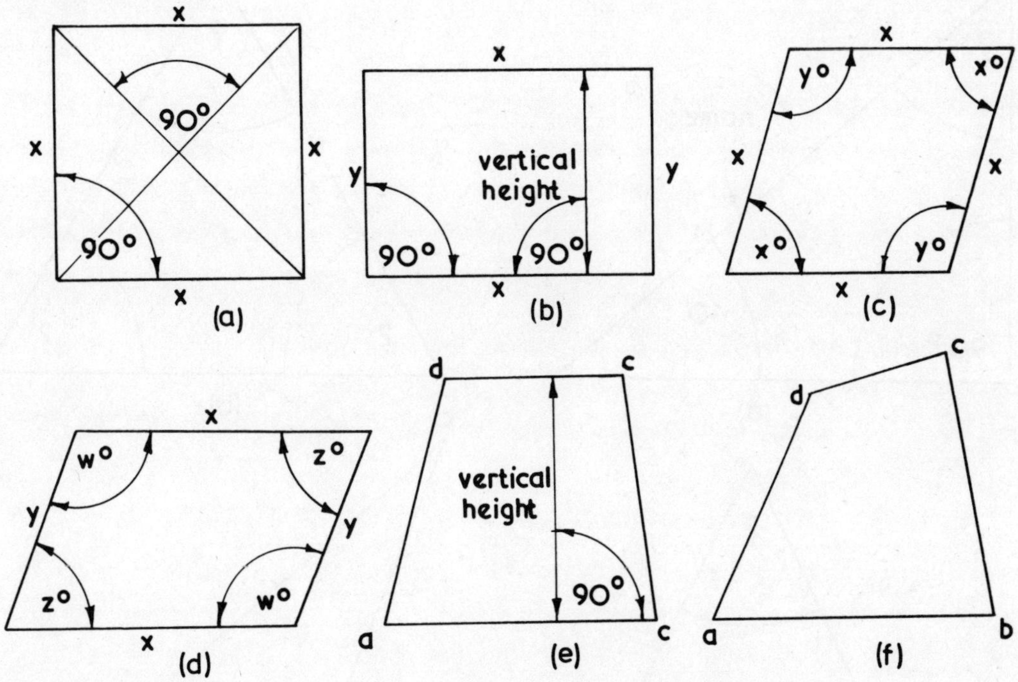

QUADRILATERAL - ITS DEFINITION	ITS NAME
all sides and opposite angles equal	
all sides and all angles equal	
sides and angles unequal	
opposite sides and all angles equal	
opposite sides and opposite angles equal	
has two sides parallel	

Figure 14.26

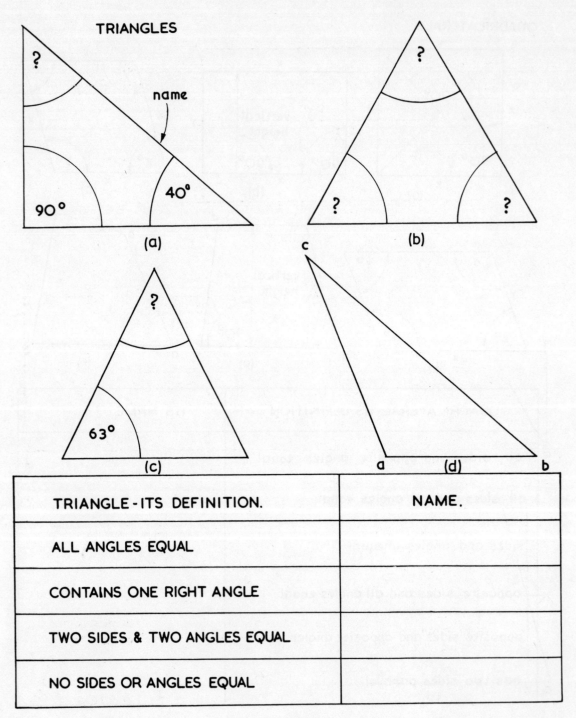

Figure 14.27

AREAS

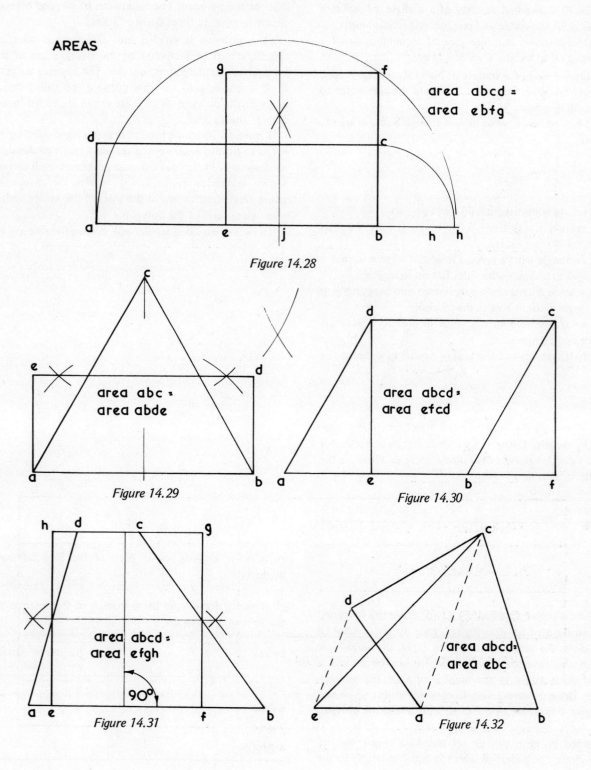

area abcd =
area ebfg

Figure 14.28

area abc =
area abde

Figure 14.29

area abcd =
area efcd

Figure 14.30

area abcd =
area efgh

90°

Figure 14.31

area abcd =
area ebc

Figure 14.32

Figure 14.29 shows that the area of a triangle is equal to a rectangle with the same base and one-half its vertical height.

Figure 14.30 shows that the area of a rhombus or of a rhomboid is equal to its base x vertical height.

To obtain the area of a trapezoid, bisect its vertical height. The bisecting line gives points on the figure through which to draw vertical lines (figure 14.31).

Figure 14.32 shows how to draw a triangle equal in area to a trapezium.

Problems

1. Draw a square with diagonals 60 mm long.
2. Draw a rectangle with base 75 mm long and with diagonals drawn with the 30° set square.
3. Draw a rectangle with a vertical height of 40 mm so that it is equal in area to a square with sides 70 mm in length.
4. Draw a scalene triangle on a base line 65 mm long and then draw a rectangle equal in area to the triangle.
5. Draw any trapezoid which is equal in area to a rectangle with 70 mm and 50 mm sides.
6. Draw any trapezium and also a square equal to its area.

Regular polygons

Regular polygons are figures with more than four straight sides all equal in length. Each polygon has its own name; for instance, a ten-sided polygon is called a decagon. What are the names of those mentioned below?

Number of sides	Name of polygon
5	
6	
7	
8	

The method shown in figure 14.33 for drawing a five-sided polygon can be used for drawing polygons of any number of sides. a — 5 is the length of the sides. Draw the semi-circle O — 5 with the radius a — 5. Divide this semi-circle into a number of parts equal to the number of sides the polygon must have. Draw a second side from a — 2. Bisect a — 5 and a — 2 to give the centre of the circle into which the polygon will fit.

A six-sided polygon can be set out in a simple way by drawing a circle, the radius of which is equal in length to the sides of the polygon. The radius can be stepped off round the circumference six times (figure 14.34).

If a polygon is divided into triangles, as seen in figure 14.35, it will be seen that all the triangles are of the same type, either equilateral or isosceles. The angle at the apex of all these triangles can, for this purpose, be called the internal angle of the polygon. If all these angles are added together the total is always 360°.

Figure 14.36 shows how to draw an eight-sided figure when it has to fit into a square of a certain size. Draw the square and its diagonals. Place your compass point into each corner of the square and with radius o — o' (where the diagonals meet) swing arcs round to two of the sides of the square each time to give two corners of the polygon.

Draw a seven-sided regular polygon on the side a — b below.

a _____ b

How many degrees are in each of the internal angles of a heptagon?
....

How many degrees are there in each of the internal angles of the following polygons

Polygon	Number of degrees in each internal angle
5-sided	
6-sided	
7-sided	
8-sided	

REGULAR POLYGONS

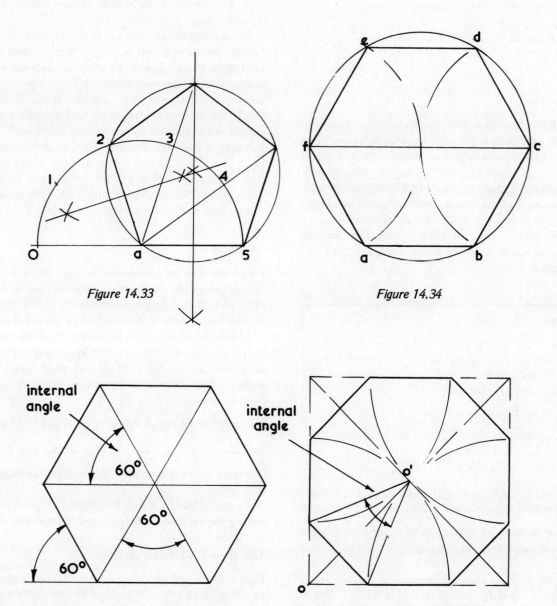

Figure 14.33

Figure 14.34

internal angle

60°

60°

60°

internal angle = $\frac{360}{6}$ = 60°

Figure 14.35

internal angle

internal angle = $\frac{360}{8}$ = 45°

Figure 14.36

Calculate the number of degrees in each of the three angles of the triangles which constitute the following

Polygon	Number of degrees in angle			Degrees (Total)
	at apex	base 1	base 2	
5-sided				
6-sided				
7-sided				
8-sided				

Irregular polygons

Figures that have more than four straight sides and these sides are not all the same length are called irregular polygons. Much information must be given before an irregular polygon can be constructed.

Four examples appear in figure 14.37 and below each example is stated part of the information given before the polygon could be drawn. Fill in the missing information.

There are many other ways of constructing irregular polygons one of which is shown below. Complete the figure using your own dimensions.

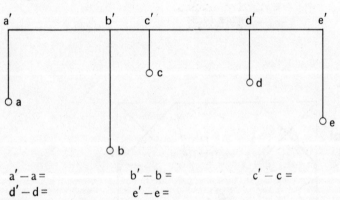

$a' - a =$ $b' - b =$ $c' - c =$
$d' - d =$ $e' - e =$

These figures can also be divided into a number of triangles which will not be similar, nor will the internal angles be equal.

Calculate the number of degrees in the remaining internal angle of the following irregular polygons.

IRREGULAR POLYGON	No. OF DEGREES IN INTERNAL ANGLES								TOTAL No. OF DEGREE
	angle 1	2	3	4	5	6	7	8	
pentagon	70	80	65	65	?				
hexagon	60	55	72	68	40	?			
heptagon	45	50	61	56	62	48	?		
octagon	32	46	50	36	28	20	20	?	

The circle

The circle is an area which is surrounded by a line called its circumference. (See pp. 132–3.)

Any point on its circumference is exactly the same distance from the centre of the circle as any other point on the circumference.

The circumference of a circle can be constructed to pass through any three points as long as these are not in a straight line (figure 14.38). Bisect the distances between each pair of points to obtain centre of circle (o).

Normals and Tangents Two examples appear in figures 14.39 and 14.40. In figure 14.39 two lines at right angles to one another are connected by an arc, and figure 14.40 shows two lines with a 60° angle between them which are also connected by an arc. (Note that normals, at right angles to each line, must be drawn at each end of the curve to give the centre.)

Continuous curves (figure 14.41) are built up with a series of arcs, each pair having a common normal.

The ellipse

The ellipse may be constructed in many ways. Some methods are considered to be more suitable for use in the drawing office and other methods are commonly used in the workshop. At least one of each of these should be learned thoroughly.

The ellipse is set out on two lines, called the major axis and the minor axis. Accuracy is most important if a true ellipse is to be set out correctly. The axes must bisect each other exactly. The curve can be drawn freehand or by some mechanical means.

The two methods shown in figures 14.42 and 14.43 are

.... and ....

Figure 14.44 shows how the focal points of an ellipse are obtained.

In figure 14.45 $a - b$ is the major axis of an ellipse and F_1 and F_2 are the focal points. Construct the ellipse.

The ellipse – workshop methods

Figure 14.46 shows a popular workshop method for constructing a true ellipse. It is called the *trammel method*.

If the lengths of the axes are known, a trammel (slip of paper, cardboard, plywood, etc.) must be obtained; mark on it, from one end, half the lengths of the major and minor axes. By placing the marks on the trammel on the two axes as shown in the illustration and repeating this in various positions, the pointed end of the trammel will pass along the curve of the ellipse.

IRREGULAR POLYGONS

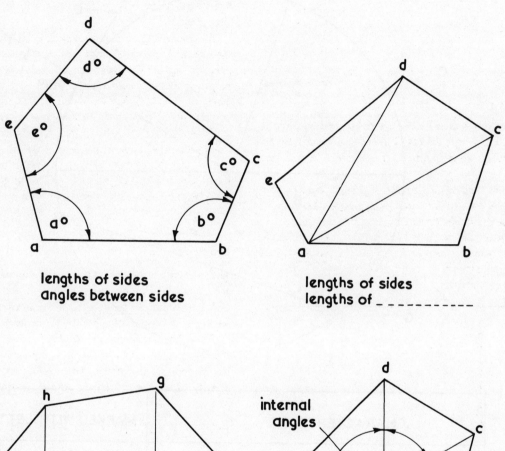

lengths of sides
angles between sides

lengths of sides
lengths of _ _ _ _ _ _ _ _ _ _

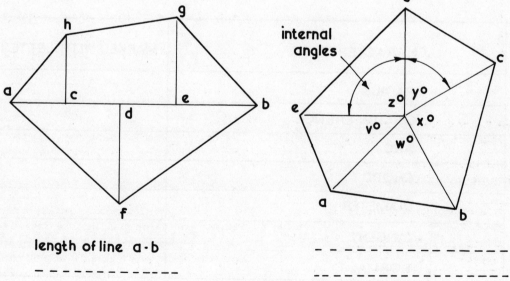

internal angles

length of line a·b

_ _ _ _ _ _ _ _ _ _ _ _ _

_ _ _ _ _ _ _ _ _ _ _ _ _ _ _ _ _ _

_ _ _ _ _ _ _ _ _ _ _ _ _ _ _ _ _ _

Figure 14.37

THE CIRCLE

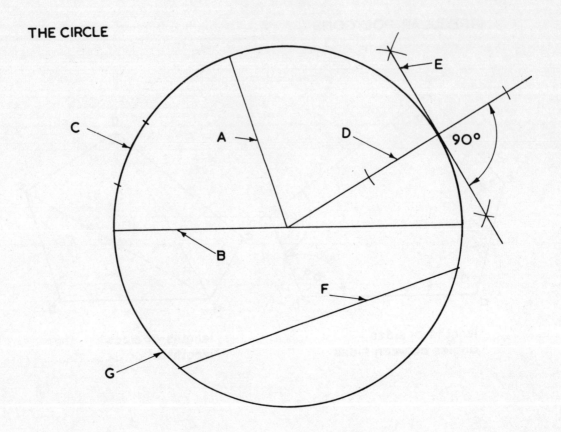

CHARACTERISTIC	MARKED WITH LETTER
RADIUS	
CIRCUMFERENCE	
ARC	
CHORD	
DIAMETER	
TANGENT	
NORMAL	

THE CIRCLE

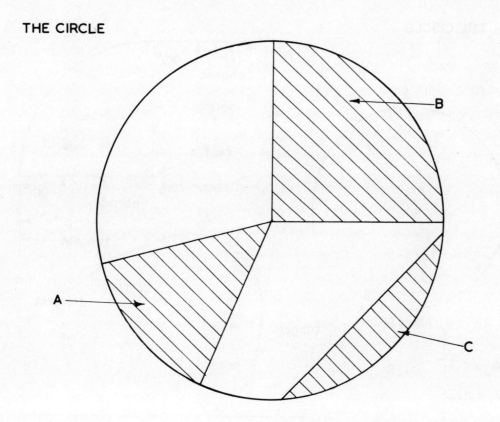

CHARACTERISTIC	MARKED WITH LETTER
	A
	B
	C

THE CIRCLE

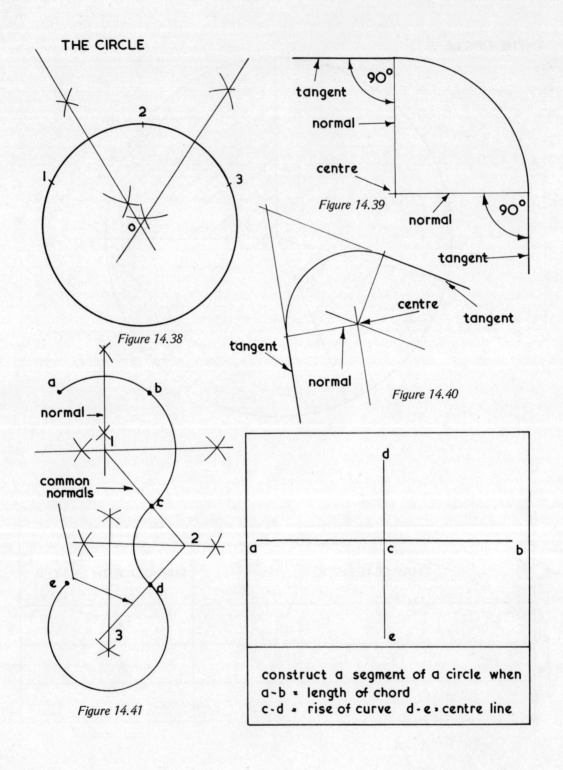

Figure 14.38

Figure 14.39

Figure 14.40

Figure 14.41

construct a segment of a circle when
a-b = length of chord
c-d = rise of curve   d-e = centre line

THE ELLIPSE

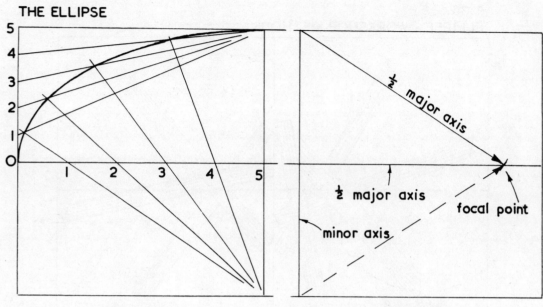

Figure 14.42

Figure 14.44

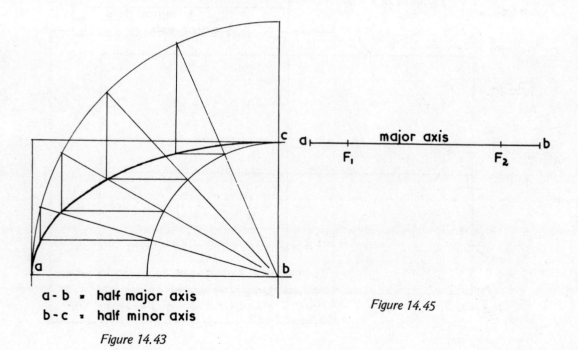

a - b = half major axis
b - c = half minor axis

Figure 14.43

Figure 14.45

ELLIPSE - WORKSHOP METHODS

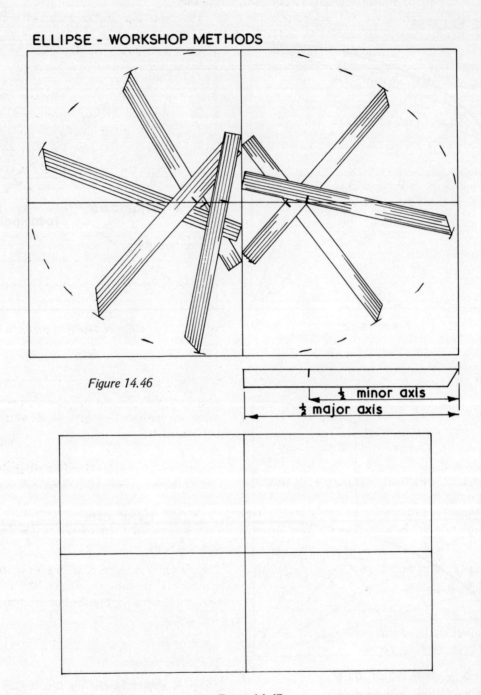

Figure 14.46

½ minor axis

½ major axis

Figure 14.47

In the rectangle shown in figure 14.47 construct an ellipse by some other mechanical means and then construct a normal and a tangent at any point on the curve. It is not possible to draw two ellipses so that their curves are running parallel with one another.

Show, also, in figure 14.47 how you would draw a curve to run parallel to the ellipse already constructed.

SOLID GEOMETRY

Geometrical solids

A thorough knowledge of solid geometry is important to carpenters, joiners and woodcutting machinists because a large percentage of their work is based on these solids.

A prism is a solid which ....

....

....

A pyramid is a solid which ....

....

....

A cylinder is a solid which ....

....

....

Before drawing details of carpentry or joinery work, the student will be taught how to draw plans and elevations and to do this, geometrical solids are used. This type of drawing is called orthographic projection and, as mentioned above, three methods are used for producing these drawings, namely, 1st angle projection, 3rd angle projection, and a combination of these two.

What is the advantage of being able to construct orthographic projections of an object? ....

....

Three geometrical solids are illustrated in figure 14.48. Sketch the solids indicated in the spaces provided.

Introduction to orthographic projections

Only an elementary knowledge of orthographic projections is required at this stage in the course and the following paragraphs aim to give an understanding of this type of drawing.

The planes of projection are shown in figure 14.49.

These planes consist of three surfaces placed in the vertical and horizontal positions — the fourth surface has been omitted to enable the details to be clearly seen. A solid block has been placed in the angles set up by the surfaces. By projecting downwards, backwards and sideways, the orthographic projections of the block can be obtained. The drawings at the bottom show the views of the block thus obtained.

You were asked to state in what angle the drawings on the last page had been constructed. What did you look for to decide on your answer? ....

....

....

....

....

....

What are the other two angles of projection?

(i) ....

(ii) ....

The front elevation and side elevation of a shaped rectangular prism are illustrated in figure 14.50. What angle of projection has been used?
....

Why have two lines in the side elevation been drawn as broken lines? ....

....

Complete the illustrations by drawing the plan and the other side elevation.

The elevation and plan of another prism which has an inclined top surface are shown in figure 14.51. You are required to draw the development of the four surfaces around the prism to the right of the elevation.

The square pyramid

Although not included in the first section of the syllabus, it is thought that a limited knowledge of one of the methods used for the development of surfaces should be included in this chapter.

Figure 14.52 shows the plan and elevation of a square

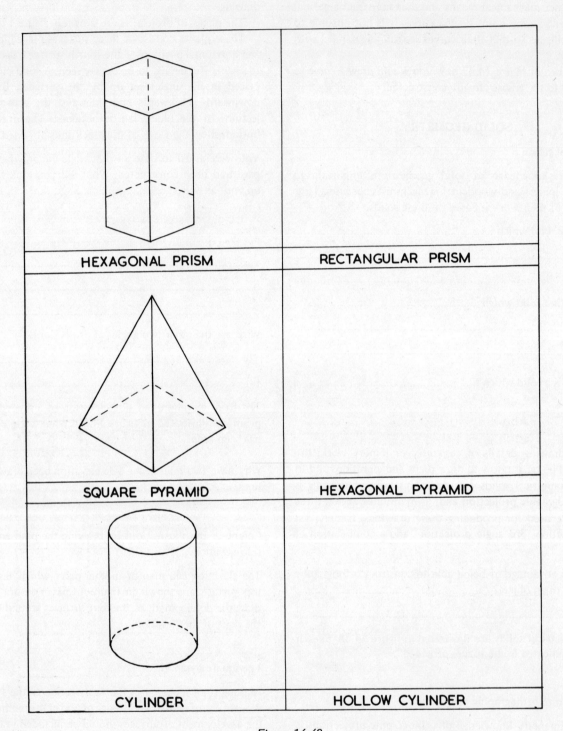

HEXAGONAL PRISM	RECTANGULAR PRISM
SQUARE PYRAMID	HEXAGONAL PYRAMID
CYLINDER	HOLLOW CYLINDER

Figure 14.48

PLANES OF PROJECTION

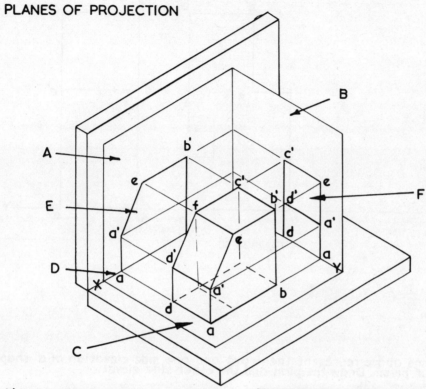

Above are the planes of projection, each part being represented by a letter. Show, on right, what each letter is.

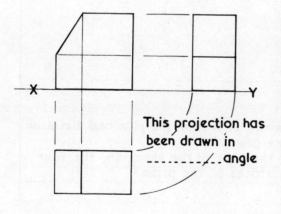

This projection has been drawn in _ _ _ _ _ _ _ _ _ _ angle

PLANES OF PROJECTION DRAWING PART	SHOWN BY LETTER
HORIZONTAL PLANE	
FRONT ELEVATION	
GROUND LINE	
VERTICAL PLANE	
SIDE ELEVATION	
SIDE VERTICAL PLANE	

Figure 14.49

PRISMS

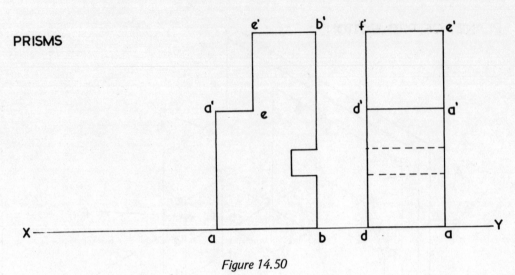

Figure 14.50

The drawings above represent the front and one side elevation of a shaped rectangular prism. Draw the plan and the other side elevation.

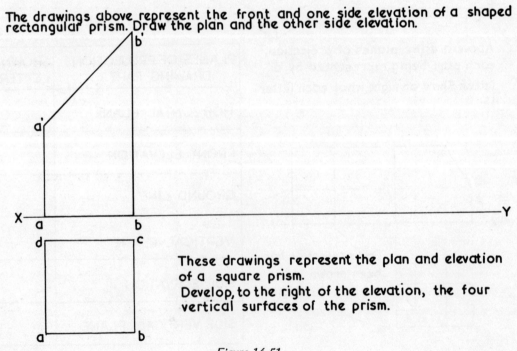

These drawings represent the plan and elevation of a square prism.
Develop, to the right of the elevation, the four vertical surfaces of the prism.

Figure 14.51

SQUARE PYRAMID

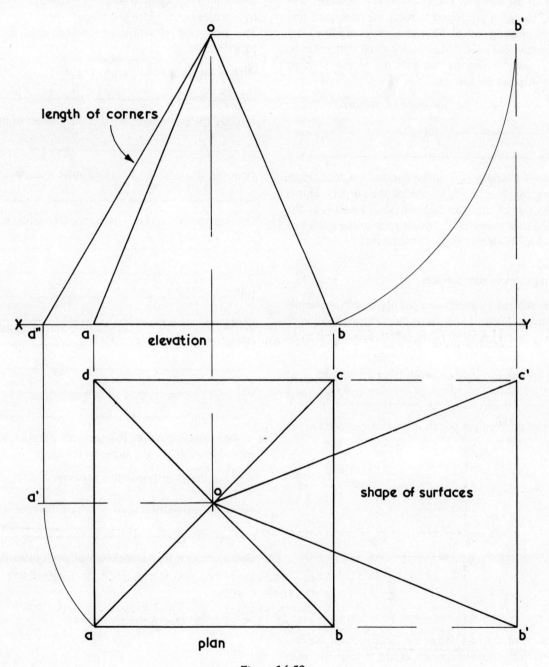

Figure 14.52

pyramid. To the right of the illustrations, a method of developing the shape of one of the sides of the pyramid is indicated. Neither the plan nor the elevation indicate the shape of the surfaces — they have to be developed. Take the surface b — c — o. With the compass point in o, in the elevation, and radius o — b, swing an arc round to meet the horizontal line drawn from o to give point b′. Then drop a vertical line from b′ to meet the two horizontal lines from c and b in the plan to give points b′ and c′. Draw the two lines o — b′ and o — c′ to complete the shape of the surface.

Explain why o — b′ — c′ is the true shape of the surface...........

....

....

The lines o — b′ and o — c′ can be checked for true length by developing the true length of one of the corners. This is shown to the left of the plan and elevation. From o in the plan, swing point a round to a′. Project a′ up to the x — y line and join a″ to o. This is the length of the corners.

Development of simple roof surfaces

Practical geometrical examples are usually based on simple geometrical solids. Figure 14.53 shows the plan and elevation of a gable roof — the type of roof found at present on most houses.

Indicate the geometrical solid on which this roof is based

....

Make an isometric freehand sketch of this form of solid in the space below.

The elevation of the roof shows the inclination of the two surfaces. This inclination is known as the pitch. The plan shows the length of the two surfaces. Line o — o′ represents the centre of the roof and the position of the ridge. This line is

also the hinge line when the two surfaces are swung into the horizontal positions of a′ — o and o — b′ in the elevation. To develop surface a — o — o′ — d drop a vertical line from a′ in the elevation to meet the horizontal lines brought out from a and d in the plan. Remember a — d must move outwards at right angles to the hinge line o — o′

The plan and elevation of another roof is illustrated in figure 14.54.

What is the name of this type of roof?

....

Measure the pitch angle. What is the number of degrees?

....

How can this pitch be described apart from that shown above?

....

Develop the two surfaces of the roof. Describe the steps taken.

(i) ....

....

(ii) ....

....

(iii) ....

....

(iv) ....

....

When developing the two surfaces, points a, b, c and d must move outwards at right angles to the hinge line.

Which is the hinge line in this drawing? ....

Name the geometrical solid on which this roof is based.

....

Below, make a freehand sketch of a side elevation of the roof.

DEVELOPMENT OF ROOF SURFACES

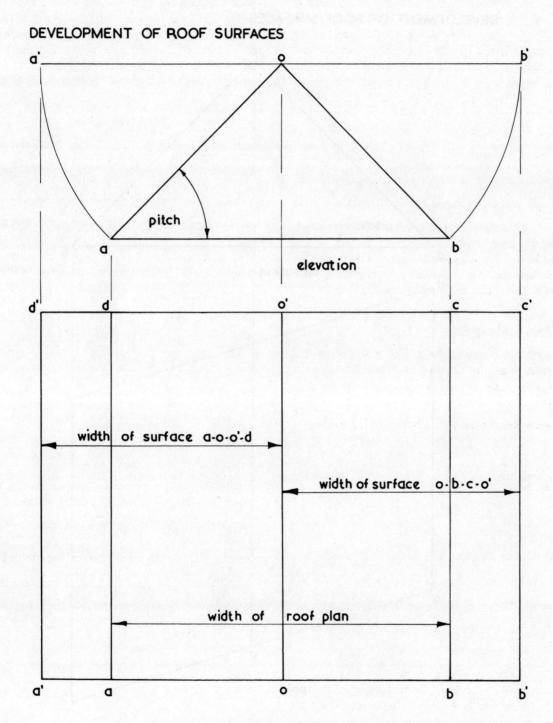

Figure 14.53

DEVELOPMENT OF ROOF SURFACES

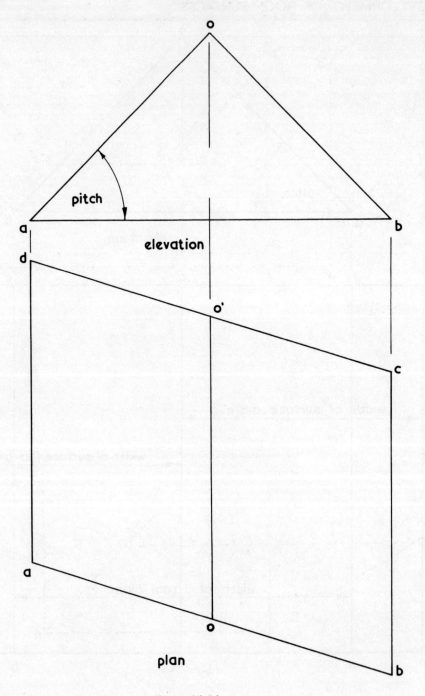

Figure 14.54

DEVELOPMENT OF ROOF SURFACES

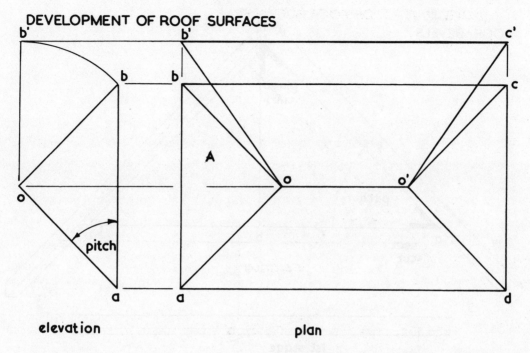

elevation   plan

Figure 14.55

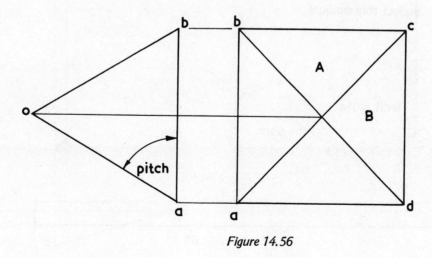

Figure 14.56

ROOF BEVELS

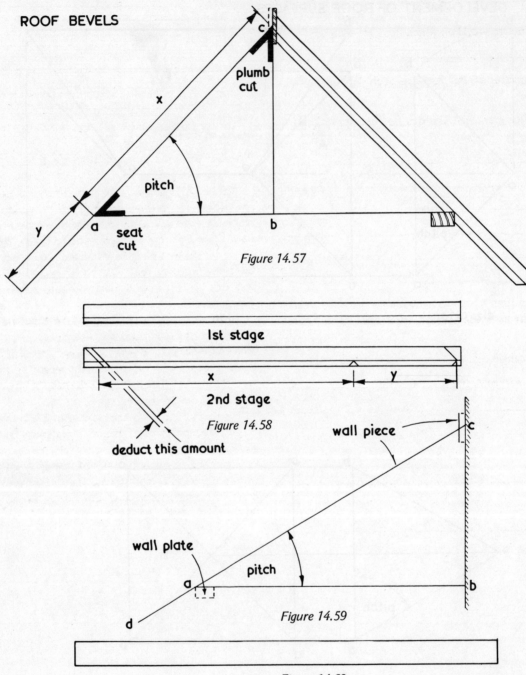

Figure 14.57

1st stage

2nd stage

Figure 14.58

deduct this amount

wall piece

wall plate

pitch

Figure 14.59

Figure 14.60

Figure 14.55 shows the plan and elevation of a hipped roof, all surfaces being inclined at the same angle. This fact is established by noting that the surfaces in the plan are all of the same width.

Indicate the geometrical solid on which this roof is based

....

One of the surfaces of this roof has been developed. The hinge line is o — o′.

Develop the surface marked A and describe the steps taken to achieve this.

(i) ....

....

(ii) ....

....

(iii) ....

....

The plan and elevation of a roof suitable for a small, square construction, such as a shed, kiosk, etc., appears in figure 14.56.

Measure the pitch angle ....

Develop surfaces marked A and B and describe the steps taken.

(i) ....

....

(ii) ....

....

(iii) ....

....

Develop the length of one of the corners.

Describe how this was done ....

....

....

....

....

Simple roof bevels

Probably the most simple roof to construct is the gable roof already mentioned above.

Figure 14.57 shows a section through a gable roof, the right-hand side showing the position of a common rafter in relation to the wall plate and ridge board. Note that a line has been placed on the rafter to pass through the top outside corner of the wall plate to terminate at c on the centre line of the ridge board or roof. On the left-hand side is shown only that line which passes through the top outside corner of the wall plate.

Distance x is the length of the rafter from the centre line of the roof to the wall plate. Distance y is the length of the rafter from the wall plate down to the end of the overhang of the eaves. Figure 14.58 shows how the length of the rafter is set out. Remember that half the thickness of the ridge must be deducted from the top end.

Figure 14.59 shows a line drawing of a lean-to roof, pitched at 30°. The positions of the wall, wallpiece (ridge) and wall plate are shown.

Figure 14.54 shows the piece of timber on which the length of the rafters is to be marked. Indicate how this should be done, showing and naming the bevels to be cut and the amount to be deducted at the top.